The Tongue of Angels

The Tongue of Angels

The Mary Marcy Reader

EDITED BY

Frederick C. Giffin

SELINSGROVE: Susquehanna University Press
LONDON AND TORONTO: Associated University Presses

Associated University Presses
440 Forsgate Drive
Cranbury, NJ 08512

Associated University Presses
25 Sicilian Avenue
London WC1A 2QH, England

Associated University Presses
P.O. Box 488, Port Credit
Mississauga, Ontario
Canada L5G 4M2

The paper used in this publication meets the requirements of the American National Standard for Permanence of Paper for Printed Library Materials Z39.48-1984.

Library of Congress Cataloging-in-Publication Data

Marcy, Mary, 1877–1922.
  The tongue of angels.

  Bibliography: p.
  Includes index.
  1. Communism—United States.   2. Labor and laboring classes—United States.   I. Giffin, Frederick C., 1938–   . II. Title.
HX84.M28A25   1988   335.43'0973   87-42930
ISBN 0-941664-91-0 (alk. paper)

Printed in the United States of America

If I had the tongue of angels, I would sing the story of the Working People!

—Mary E. Marcy,
"Letters of a Pork Packer's Stenographer"

Contents

Preface

THE present anthology is intended to provide the general reading public as well as students of the American left with representative selections from the published works of Mary E. Marcy, a talented but little remembered radical editor and writer whose career coincided with the heyday of the Socialist Party of America and of the radical labor organization the Industrial Workers of the World. An introductory essay briefly describes the history and influence of these two organizations and outlines the major events of Marcy's professional life. To further assist the reader, the selections themselves are prefaced by short commentaries that seek to clarify their intent and to place them in historical context.

Unfortunately, a satisfactory biography of Marcy will never be written. A dearth of information renders such an endeavor impossible. We know very little about her personality, her husband, or her family life, and we are privy to virtually none of the details of her friendships with radical associates. The most useful sources of information on her—all of them woefully inadequate—are the "News and Views" section in each issue of the monthly *International Socialist Review* (1900–18), the autobiography of Ralph Chaplin, *Wobbly: The Rough-and-Tumble Story of an American Radical* (Chicago: University of Chicago Press, 1948), and *Mary Marcy* (Chicago: Charles H. Kerr & Co., 1922), a brief memorial pamphlet written by Jack Carney, one of the organizers of the Communist Labor Party and an editor of its theoretical organ, the *Class Struggle*. There are no Mary Marcy papers. Most of her personal records and correspondence were destroyed in a fire at Charles H. Kerr & Company, the Chicago publishing house where she was employed from 1908 until her death in 1922; the remainder were seized by agents of the Justice Department during the so-called "great red scare" of 1919–20 and were subsequently lost or discarded. There are no surviving relatives, friends, or colleagues who might share their recollections of her. The Chicago Historical Society and that city's famed Newberry Library have no information on her. Neither the Socialist Party of America Papers at Duke University, the Industrial Workers of the World materials in the Joseph A. Labadie Collection at the University of Michigan, the Archives of Labor History and Urban Affairs at Wayne State University, the collections of socialist and labor materials at the State Historical Society of Wisconsin and at New York's Tamiment Library, nor the papers of Ralph Chaplin and others of her comrades in the radical movement include enlightening references to her. Numerous other potential sources of information about Marcy's life, many of them suggested by leading scholars of American radicalism who kindly volunteered their assistance, prove equally barren. Most of what we can know of Mary Marcy concerns the nature of her radical outlook and must be gleaned from reading her published writings.

Happily, there are an abundance of readily available works on the radical milieu in which she lived and worked. Among them, the following were the most valuable in preparing this anthology: Melvyn Dubofsky, *We Shall Be All: A History of the Industrial Workers of the World* (Chicago: Quadrangle Books, 1969); Joseph R. Conlin, ed., *The American Radical Press, 1880–1980*, 2 vols., (Westport, Connecticut: Greenwood Press, 1974); Ira Kipnis, *The American Socialist Movement, 1897–1912* (New York: Columbia University Press, 1952); Patrick Renshaw, *The Wobblies: The Story of Syndicalism in the United States* (Garden City, New York: Doubleday, 1967); Walter B. Rideout, *The Radical Novel in the United States, 1900–1954* (Cambridge: Harvard University Press, 1956); David A. Shannon, *The Socialist Party of America: A History* (New York: Macmillan, 1955); and James Weinstein, *The Decline of Socialism in America, 1912–1925* (New York: Monthly Review Press, 1967). Other studies that have proved especially useful are Mari Jo Buhl, *Women and American Socialism, 1870–1920* (Urbana: University of Illinois Press, 1981); Peter Carlson, *Roughneck: The Life and Times of Big Bill Haywood* (New York: W. W. Norton, 1983); Joseph R. Conlin, *Big Bill Haywood and the Radical Union Movement* (Syracuse: Syracuse University Press, 1969); William M. Dick, *Labor and Socialism in America: The Gompers Era* (Port Washington, New York: Kennikat Press, 1972); Theodore Draper, *The Roots of American Communism* (New York: Viking Press, 1957); Ray Ginger, *The Bending Cross: A Biography of Eugene V. Debs* (New Brunswick: Rutgers University Press, 1949); Irving Howe, *Socialism and America* (New York: Harcourt Brace Jovanovich, 1985); Sally M. Miller, ed., *Flawed Liberation: Socialism and Feminism* (Westport, Connecticut: Greenwood Press, 1981); and Alice Wexler, *Emma Goldman: An Intimate Life* (New York: Pantheon Books, 1984).

While I am solely responsible for editing this volume, I owe a special debt to Neil K. Basen, who rendered invaluable assistance in locating copies of Marcy's publications. Thanks are also due Arizona State University for a faculty grant-in-aid that supported the research for this anthology.

The Tongue of Angels

Introduction

IF it may be said that there was a golden age of the American Left, most historians would agree that it fell within the period between the reelection of William McKinley in 1900 and the victory of Warren G. Harding in 1920. During these opening decades of a new century, the American Left was dominated by two organizations, both of which attracted nationwide attention and received a remarkable degree of success: the Socialist Party of America and the radical labor organization the Industrial Workers of the World (IWW).

Founded in Indianapolis, Indiana, in July 1901, the Socialist Party of America advocated abolishing the capitalist system of private ownership and replacing it with a cooperative system based on public ownership and the democratic control of the means of production and distribution. Far from being a political sect with rigid discipline and strict ideological uniformity, the party was a broad, democratic organization representing all varieties of leftist conviction. Structurally, it was highly decentralized; it was a federation of separate state bodies, each capable of doing much as it wished, with very limited direction from the party's National Executive Committee headquartered in Chicago. State organizations commonly concentrated their attention on grass-roots problems. For example, party organizations in the west were concerned primarily with issues involving miners and farmers, while in New York, attention was focused on the problems of workers in the urban slums.

Although diversity was the basis of the party's strength, it also led to the development of two wings within the organization—and thereby provided the seed for the party's decline during the several years following the Bolshevik revolution of 1917 in Russia. The right wing, which held power in the party after the election of Milwaukee Socialist Victor Berger to Congress in 1910, tended to dominate in New York, Pennsylvania, and Wisconsin. The left wing was found primarily in Indiana, Michigan, Ohio, and west of the Mississippi. Central to this division was a disagreement over whether socialism would come about gradually or through revolution. Whereas right-wing spokesmen, or "evolutionists" as they were called, regarded liberal economic reforms as desirable and favored a step-by-step progression toward socialism through worker education and the ballot box, the left wing believed that attempts to improve the condition of the working class within the framework of capitalism only postponed the necessary revolution. From the perspective of the party's left-wing adherents, a majority of whom were members or supporters of the IWW, the evolutionists were "Slow-cialists," willing to sacrifice their principles for a few votes. To the right wing, on the other hand, the revolutionaries were "impossibilists," who frightened away potential supporters of the Socialist party with irresponsible rhetoric.

Until 1912, the trouble brewing between the right-wing and left-wing factions was overshadowed by the party's continuous growth and wide influence on the nation's political life. Membership increased fourfold between 1901 and 1908, and grew even more dramatically during the next several years, reaching in 1912 an all-time high of nearly 118,000. In that same year, Eugene V. Debs, the party's presidential candidate, polled approximately 6 percent of the total vote; Socialists controlled thirty-three American cities, including Milwaukee; Berkeley, California; Butte, Montana; and Flint, Michigan; Max Hayes, a comrade from Cleveland, won a third of the vote for president of the American Federation of Labor against the powerful incumbent Samuel Gompers; and there were 323 Socialist periodical publications issued in the United States. The most successful and influential of the periodicals, the weekly *Appeal to Reason,* published in Kansas, had a circulation of over a half-million. It and *Wilshire's Magazine* enjoyed the largest circulations, respectively, of all Socialist periodicals in the world.

Then, at this highpoint of Socialist party strength and influence, the dispute between right- and left-wing elements came to a head. At the party's 1912 convention, the Right introduced a motion, proposed by Victor Berger, that anyone who advocated "violence, sabotage, and crime" should be denied membership in the party. Berger's motion, which passed by a majority of more than two-to-one, was clearly aimed at comrades belonging to the IWW, party members whose endorsement of revolution and sabotage presumably was alienating the very middle-class reformist elements to whom the right was appealing with increasing success. The following year, William D. "Big Bill" Haywood, prominent IWW member and titular head of the left wing, was driven from his post on the National Executive Committee because of the charge that he advocated violent sabotage.

In the aftermath of Haywood's recall, Socialist party membership declined drastically, as considerable numbers of left-wing adherents departed its ranks with no compensating influx of "evolutionists." Moreover, in 1913 and 1914, most of the electoral gains of earlier years were wiped out. And when Berger and other members of the right wing succeeded in 1916 in replacing the "revolutionist" Debs with a moderate Socialist as presidential candidate, the party's nominee won less than two-thirds of Debs's 1912 total.

In 1917, with America's entry into World War I, the party seemed to be recovering, no doubt largely because it played an extremely important role as the focal point for all who objected to the conflict and their country's participation in it. During the early period of United States involvement, enough Americans agreed with the party's stand that it did well at the polls. Not only did Socialists win election to several state legislatures and nearly succeed in capturing the municipal administrations of a number of large cities, but Victor Berger was again elected to Congress. However, as the war ground on, the Socialists were hard hit by the policies of an administration whose mounting intolerance of dissent led it to prosecute actively more than two thousand people, many for simply speaking against the conflict—among them Berger and Debs. By the war's end, almost a third of the party's National Executive Committee was behind bars. Equally as damaging, vigilantes pursued the administration's case out of court, conducting raids on Socialist party headquarters and physically attacking presumed as well as actual Socialists. A by-no-means-atypical outburst of vigilantism occurred at Rutgers University, where an antiwar Socialist student who refused to take part in a Liberty Loan rally was stripped, covered with molasses and feathers, and paraded through the streets of New Brunswick.

Attacked from without, the Socialist party soon split from within as the result of bitter internecine struggles engendered by the Bolsheviks' success in Russia. Initially, every faction of the American Left identified with the Bolsheviks, including right-wing Socialists who had denounced the doctrine of violence. "Evolutionists" like Morris Hillquit, the Socialist candidate for mayor of New York in 1917, defended the "dictatorship of the proletariat" as democratic, and even Debs, among the gentlest of radicals, announced: "From the crown of my head to the soles of my feet I am a Bolshevik, and proud of it." Within a short time, however, differences over the Bolshevik revolution's relevance to the United States prompted a fierce struggle for control of the party. After the Communist International (Comintern), born in Moscow in March 1919, ordered every socialist party in the world to split from its right-wing factions, the left-wing of the American party attempted to capture the organization's machinery. In the fierce struggle that ensued, the party's right-wing leadership first moved to expel the entire Michigan party as well as seven foreign-language federations, then declared null and void recent elections for a new National Executive Committee that gave a decisive majority to the left wing. Disgusted, left-wing leaders deserted the party and formed a separate communist organization, which immediately split into two factions, the Communist Party and the smaller Communist Labor Party. Not only was American radicalism now split between Socialists and Communists, but the former lost their authenticity as a movement of radical action. By 1920 there were less than 27,000 dues-paying Socialists. And things were to get worse for the party that had for two decades provided a consistent alternative to corporate capitalism in the form of democratic socialism. In 1922 membership fell below 12,000. Oklahoma, which had polled more Socialist votes in 1914 than any other state, had a mere 72 members in 1922, while only New York, Wisconsin, Pennsylvania, and Massachusetts had as many as one thousand. Although the Socialist party experienced some revival in the 1930s, during the Great Depression, it never regained its popular base or the electoral appeal of earlier years.

Properly speaking, the Socialist Party of America was a movement not of, but on behalf of, the working class. While it claimed to speak for the workers and to articulate their needs, its doctrines and tactics were developed by intellectuals and party leaders. In contrast, the IWW was the embodiment of a working class that spoke on its own behalf and battled to advance its own class interests.

Founded in Chicago in June 1905 by a varied group of unionists, radical journalists, and Socialists who resolved that "the working class and the employing class have nothing in common"[1] and were distressed by the more moderate and exclusivist American Federation of Labor, the IWW sought to organize skilled and unskilled workers into huge industrial unions that would employ direct economic action to take control of industry and destroy capitalism. Composed largely of the migratory lumbermen, construction workers, harvesters, and miners of the west and the unskilled factory workers of the east, the Wobblies (as the IWW's members were commonly known) were tough, boisterous, defiant, and addicted to verbal violence. Under the aegis of "direct action," "sabotage," and the "general strike," they conducted about 150 strikes in the decade following their organization's formation. In 1912, when the IWW enrolled about a hundred thousand members and probably reached the peak of its influence, it won a dramatic, long-fought textile strike in Lawrence, Massachusetts. But success also brought enemies. Some of the latter confined their hatred to harsh diatribes, such as the *San Diego Tribune* editor who branded the Wobblies "the waste material of creation," and called for them to be "drained off into the sewers of oblivion, there to rot in cold obstruction like any other excrement."[2] Others eschewed words in favor of action. IWW agitator Carlo Tresca was gunned down by an unknown political assassin; Wesley Everest, a northwestern lumberman, was castrated then riddled with bullets by members of the American Legion; and Wobbly leader Frank Little was lynched by six Montana vigilantes.

Although the ideology of the IWW derived much of its spirit from Socialist party doctrine, the two organizations came into conflict more frequently than they agreed. Contemptuous, for the most part, of politics, and contemptuous, without exception, of reformers, the Wobblies disdained Socialist efforts to transform the capitalist state into a cooperative commonwealth through the ballot box and urged defiance of the law and "real" revolution. After William D. "Big Bill" Haywood was recalled from the Socialist Party's National Executive Committee in 1913, the IWW was still seen as the hope of the working class—the revolution fleshed—by some left-wing Socialists, but most Socialists and Wobblies went their separate ways.

Ironically, while the IWW preached antimilitarism and antipatriotism as basic principles, actively campaigned against American entry into World War I, and declined to join the American Federation of Labor in a no-strike pledge, it did not play a significant role in the antiwar activities that followed United States' intervention. After April 1917, the IWW concentrated its energies on organizing miners, lumber workers, and harvest hands. Nonetheless, there was a widespread public belief that it meant to hinder the war effort at all costs, and the government responded accordingly. The union's strikes were broken, many of its alien members were deported, and the majority of its prominent officials and spokesmen were prosecuted and imprisoned.

The prosecutions conducted by the government continued after the war and critically impaired the effectiveness of the organization. Yet, as was the case with the Socialist Party of America, it was the Bolsheviks' victory in Russia and the divisiveness that dramatic event engendered among the union's membership that deprived the IWW of its vitality and its influence as a model for social change. At first, most of the organization's members sympathized with the Bolshevik revolution. In its 8 December 1917 number, for example, the IWW publication *Defense News Bulletin* announced that "in broad essentials" the Bolsheviks "stand for about the same thing in Russia as our IWW stands for in America," specifically workers' control of industry through industrial unions. But before long a bitter controversy arose over the issue of political as opposed to economic means of ushering in the sought-after "Workers' Co-Operative Republic." In 1920, the Comintern called upon the Wobblies to relinquish their traditional apolitical stand in light of the new revolutionary situation. Comintern spokesmen argued that the workers must grab political power, set up the dictatorship of the proletariat, establish a socialist state, and then gradually bring about the communization of productive power. Although the IWW rejected the Comintern's appeal, regarding the Bolshevik revolution as an unacceptable model to follow because of its emphasis on political action and state power, many Wobblies abandoned the union for the American Communist movement—most notably such influential members as Haywood, William Z. Foster, and later Elizabeth Gurley Flynn. These defections, following in the wake of government repression, took the heart out of the IWW. Despite a brief resurgence during the depression decade of the 1930s, it never really recovered. It survives to this day, no longer a true union but a skeletal organization on the fringe of American radicalism.

Debs, Haywod, Berger, and most of the other leading Socialists and Wobblies of the American Left's golden age survive to this day in the writings of historians. Their contributions to our society are available for examination by succeeding generations of Americans. Yet, countless other radicals who played important supporting roles during the heyday of the Socialist party and the IWW have been overlooked by historians. Their efforts to fulfill the Left's dream of a postcapitalist society are today all but forgotten. Such is the case of Mary E. Marcy, a small, dark-haired, square-jawed dyamo of a woman, who served for nearly a decade as an associate and then managing editor and foremost missionary of Charles H. Kerr's Chicago-based *International Socialist Review* (1900–1918). A gifted proponent of "socialism in overalls," she was acclaimed by her contemporaries in the labor movement as a skilled writer almost without equal in her ability to bring the socialist message before American workers in a manner they could both understand and appreciate. Following her death in 1922, Debs paid tribute to her as "one of the clearest minds and greatest souls" in the movement.

Born Mary Edna Tobias in Belleville, Illinois, on 8 May 1877, Mary was orphaned at an early age and, after completing high school, she assumed full responsibility for her two younger siblings, Roscoe and Inez. She supported them through their school years by working as a switchboard operator for a firm that manufactured American flags. Fortunately, Roscoe and Inez had completed their schooling by 1896, when Mary's independent spirit and growing interest in political matters caused her to lose her job. In defiance of her employer's explicit prohibitions against such actions, she had worn a William Jennings Bryan button during the Great Commoner's unsuccessful campaign for the presidency of the United States.

Learning of her dismissal and the circumstances that provoked it, the noted attorney Clarence Darrow, whose writings would later appear in the *International Socialist Review,* got her a position under William Rainey Harper, first president of the University of Chicago (1891–1906). Much to the benefit of Mary's intellectual development, Harper arranged for her to attend classes, tuition-free, during her spare hours, and she took advantage of this opportunity by studying under such luminaries as philosopher John Dewey, an adherent of pragmatism, who believed that the business of the teacher is "to re-examine and re-appraise, to accept no system as final, but to push on to new conceptions of truth."[3] For Dewey, the test of a political or social or economic institution was neither its age nor its acceptance by the respectable and contented, but rather the way in which the institution worked. The goal should always be improvement.

Following nearly three years at the University of Chicago, Mary wed Leslie H. Marcy, an aspiring young journalist, and the couple moved to Kansas City, Missouri. Leslie obtained employment at the United States Water and Steam Supply Company, while Mary worked successively for two large meat-packing firms. She was employed as a stenographer by Swift and Company from the beginning of 1902 through June 1903, and for the following eight months, she was secretary to the treasurer of Armour Company. Shortly after Mary joined the Armour firm, both she and Leslie became members of the Socialist Party of America, memberships they would maintain until 1917.

It was her experience with the meat-packers that prompted Mary's first venture into journalism. Between August 1904 and January 1905, her hard-hitting serial "Letters of a Pork Packer's Stenographer" was published in the *International Socialist Review*. She had met the journal's founder, Charles H. Kerr, the principal owner of a small but profitable cooperative publishing house specializing in translations of European socialist writers, soon after joining the Socialist party, and the two entered into a personal as well as a professional relationship, which lasted until Mary's death. College-educated, fluent in French, the son of a professor of Greek literature at the University of Wisconsin, Kerr was a quiet, studious man with sensitive features who had moved to Chicago in 1882 and worked for a Unitarian publishing house before joining with nearly eight hundred other self-declared socialists in 1886 to establish Charles H. Kerr & Company. At first the firm put out chiefly books on "free thought," but in 1899, its officials decided to issue only material concerned with the international socialist movement. In March of that year, the company published May Wood Simons's *Woman and the Social Problem,* the first number of the Pocket Library of Socialism, a series of pocket-size pamphlets covered in transparent red paper. A few months later it introduced the Library of Progress, a series mainly devoted to inexpensive reprints of the classics of Marxism. The profits of the press increased as a consequence of this new emphasis, and the number of its stockholders grew from less than 160 at the beginning of 1899 to 815 in mid-1904, by which time it had come nearer to being owned by the

Socialist Party of America than any other publishing house. Over one hundred party locals were joint owners of the company, and had a voice in its management. The firm began publication of the *International Socialist Review* in July 1900.

Marcy's attack on the meat-packing industry, appearing in the *Review* at a time when "trust busting" was much in vogue, resulted in her being subpoenaed to appear before a grand jury in Chicago as a witness of the United States government against the beef trust, described at this time by the muckraking journalist Charles Edward Russell in *Everybody's Magazine* as "a power greater than the government, greater than the courts or judges . . . superior to and independent of all authority or state or nation."[4] The trust concept was the brainchild of Samuel C. T. Dodd, the chief counsel of Standard Oil. It was a legal arrangement under which stockholders in a corporation gave their stock "in trust" to a central board of directors, the members of which were authorized to vote the stock as they desired, while the dividends on the stock continued to be paid to the shareholders, who had surrendered their stock for trust certificates. In 1882 Dodd established a trust for Standard Oil that enabled its board of directors to control from the firm's headquarters in New York City the overall policies of forty corporations. Soon the trust idea spread to other industries, resulting not only in a beef trust, but a sugar trust, and a dozen more. By the late 1880s, trusts were virtually an omnipresent feature of American industry, increasingly complained about in the press and in governmental circles. Then, beginning in the 1890s, the trusts came up with a still-more-effective means of avoiding competition: the corporate merger, a simple device by which a corporation bought up the stock of another corporation, thereby winning control of its price and other policies. As a consequence of such mergers, by 1904, when the *Review* ran the first installment of Marcy's serial, there were an estimated three hundred trusts in the United States, led by John Pierpont Morgan's United States Steel Corporation, which together owned $20 billion—over 40 percent of all the industrial wealth of the nation.

Following her testimony in Chicago, Mary returned to Kansas City and secured a position with the Associated Charities—an experience reflected in her "socialist novel" *Out of the Dump,* written several years later. Much to their credit, the Associated Charities turned a deaf ear to the meat-packers' threat that they would withdraw their annual donations unless "that Marcy woman" was fired.

As it happened, she left the Associated Charities, and Kansas City, on her own volition. Her "Letters of a Pork Packer's Stenographer" and her subsequent testimony before the grand jury had attracted considerable comment in the Chicago newspapers and, on the strength of that publicity, in 1908 she was offered an associate editorship of the *International Socialist Review.* Mary accepted the offer, becoming as well the secretary of Charles H. Kerr & Company. Her husband, Leslie, joined the Review as business manager.

From its founding at the turn of the century until shortly before the Marcys were invited to join its staff, the *International Socialist Review* was a sometimes pedantic, often difficult to comprehend journal, more likely to be read by professors than by workers. Under the direction of its first editor, Algie M. Simons, a brilliant Wisconsin Phi Beta Kappan through whom Charles Kerr had first come into touch with the Socialist party, it was published to "educate the educators," Its issues were largely devoted to discussions of Marxist theory aimed at instructing socialist intellectuals who would presumably then pass their knowledge on down to the party's rank and file. Typical of Simons's turgid approach, the three major articles in the journal's January 1908 number (the last one published under his editorship) were "The Element of Faith in Marxian Socialism," "Economic Determinism and Martyrdom," and "Planlessness of Production the Cause of Panics."

The main reason for Simons's dismissal following the release of the January 1908 number most likely was not so much that Kerr had come to regard him as a high-brow, ill-suited to edit a mass circulation magazine, as it was a difference of opinion about the proper relationship of the Socialist party to the Wobblies. Although Simons had been one of the founders of the IWW in 1905, his enthusiasm for the organization had quickly waned. Meanwhile, Kerr, who found himself increasingly attracted to the Socialist party's left wing, had come to favor a closer alliance with the IWW. Accordingly, he determined to transform the *Review* into a journal, "of, by and for the working class" and use its pages to spread "the propaganda of the revolution and the new industrial unionism."[5]

Following Simons's departure, Kerr acted as his own editor for a brief time and then turned editorial control over to the Marcys. Under their guidance—especially that of Mary, who soon established herself as the "spark plug" of the operation—the *Review* emerged as the unofficial organ of the left wing of the Socialist party, becoming a militant, flashy, copiously illustrated monthly in the thick of every major labor dispute. The most steadfast and almost the only supporter of the IWW among Socialist periodicals, it recorded the bitter conflicts waged by the Lawrence, Massachusetts, woolenworkers, the Louisiana timber laborers, and the great plains farmhands; it praised revolutionary journalist John Reed's "Pageant of the Paterson Strike," a reenactment in New York City's Madison Square Garden of the major events in the dramatic 1913 strike of silkworkers in Paterson, New Jersey; it opened its pages to

Eugene Debs's more controversial pronouncements and added the colorful and highly publicized Wobbly leader "Big Bill" Haywood to its list of contributing editors; it printed articles and poems by the Swedish-born IWW organizer and bard Joe Hill; and it devoted increasing space to articles that disapproved of "the political tactics and reformist policies of the Socialist Party leadership" and urged all "clear-headed" opponents of capitalism who were reluctant to join an organization they had come to regard as a vote-getting, office-seeking machine to enroll at once in order that the party might be set upon the proper road—that of "revolutionary" socialism.[6] Still more distinctive of the *Review*'s new radical bent, its January 1916 number included excerpts from the pamphlet *Socialism and War* by the Russian Bolsheviks Vladimir Lenin and Grigori Zinoviev—the first American publication of anything written by Lenin. The only notable exceptions to the *Review*'s missionary tone as "the fighting magazine of the working class" could be found regularly in its pages carrying advertisements, where would-be investors were promised quick returns through land speculation, and salesmen were informed of the profits to be made through peddling such products as cream separators.

If increased circulation is any index, the journal's altered approach was a resounding success. Within a year of Simons's dismissal, actual paid circulation leaped 300 percent. By July 1910 the *Review* had 27,000 readers. Six months later it claimed a circulation of 45,000; and in 1912, the year that both the Socialist party and the IWW reached the highpoint of their influence, it was selling 50,000 copies of each issue. Although the *Review*'s circulation never even remotely approached that of either the two weeklies the *Appeal to Reason* (over 50,000) and the *National Rip-Saw* (200,000) or the monthly *Wilshire's Magazine* (400,000), by 1911 it had attracted a larger readership than most of the other more than three hundred socialist periodicals published in the United States; and following the outbreak of the war in Europe it did nearly as well as the weekly *American Socialist* (60,000), the official organ of the Socialist Party of America from 1914 until 1917, when it was suppressed together with other antiwar publications.

Not surprisingly, considering its success and its impassioned support of both the party's left wing and the IWW, the revamped *Review* was not without its critics among right-wing Socialists. They saw the magazine's destruction as the best means to check the growing influence of industrial socialism. In the midst of the National Executive Committee elections of December 1911, one such critic, Robert Hunter, complaining that the *Review*'s "constant emphasis . . . on Direct Action and its apparent faith that a revolution can be evoked by Will or Force is in direct opposition to our whole philosophy,"[7] forced an official party investigation of Kerr and his varied publishing enterprises. Hunter charged that the Chicago publisher not only ran his "empire" dictatorially, but was building a machine for the purpose of subverting the Socialist party. The result of the ensuing probe was far from what Kerr's detractors had hoped for, however. The investigating committee concluded that "no Socialist publishing house has more open methods of conducting business than this one"[8] and revealed that Kerr himself was paid a mere $1,500 a year in salary, and that the employees of the *Review* worked an eight-hour day, received time-and-a-half for overtime, and even got a week's vacation with pay. Much to Hunter's embarrassment, the committee also reported that he had been a stockholder in the publishing house since 1900, that he had given his proxy to Kerr in writing "good until revoked," and that he enjoyed the right to attend in person or by proxy all stockholders' meetings and to examine the books of the company.

Mary Marcy's commitment to fulfilling Kerr's charge to fashion the *Review* into a fighting magazine "of, by and for the working class" was expressed forcibly not only through her editorial guidance, but also in her numerous articles and editorials emphasizing that socialism was the necessary alternative to a capitalist system that "rests upon robbery and sloth, poverty . . . murder and oppression."[9] Time and again she repeated the message advanced in her hard-hitting article "Are You a Socialist?" published in the August 1911 number: "SOCIALISM IS THE ONLY HOPE IN THE WORLD FOR THE WORKING CLASS."

Yet, while Mary supported the Socialist party and urged the working class to follow her example, she did not hesitate to criticize any official or other member of the party who seemed to her to be attempting to divert it from its revolutionary work into a petty and futile chase after votes and offices. Thus, in September 1911, she cautioned the *Review*'s readers to beware of Socialist politicians who declare that they intend to "serve all people." No one "can serve capitalism and the working class at the same time," she insisted.

> The man who claims to serve Capitalists and wageworkers is either unacquainted with the aims and teachings of socialism and needs a good course in revolutionary socialism, or he is a hopeless utopian who will, if permitted, lead the party into the camp of Compromise and the Enemy. . . . THE GREATEST VIRTUE OF THE REVOLUTIONIST IS LOYALTY TO THE INTERESTS OF THE WORKING CLASS. This above all things must all our PUBLIC SERVANTS possess. Without it they are the EXPLOITERS OF OUR CLASS.[10]

Given her dedication to revolutionary socialism, it is not surprising that Mary shared enthusiastically in Kerr's endorsements of the IWW, viewing the latter as an organization that was teaching the workers to exercise their actual power. In complete harmony with the definition of "Direct Action" set forth in the 2 July 1910 number of the official IWW weekly, *Solidarity,* she believed that "the strike . . . teaches working class self-reliance . . . better than anything else." The strike was in her opinion one of the greatest weapons by which laborers could secure a greater portion of the value they create. As Mary editorialized in the *Review* of April 1915, "I only know that we shall never get anywhere on our own initiative unless we revolt, unless we rebel, unless we struggle. The class war will have to be FOUGHT OUT. And every act of rebellion and revolt will make us better fighters for the overthrow of Capitalism, fighters with weapons tried and found effective. Revolt! Revolt again! And again Revolt!"[11]

But there was one kind of fighting to which Mary, like the overwhelming majority of her Socialist comrades, was unalterably opposed. "Direct action against the capitalist class may prove of great benefit to the producers of wealth," she declared in September 1915, "but direct action in capitalist wars can only mean greater poverty, misery and degradation to the workers who carry on these wars."[12] Her message in many articles and editorials appearing in the *Review* following the outbreak of hostilities in Europe was that all wars "except the class war (between the working class and those who rob them)" were fought for just one purpose: to "determine which natural trust shall be master, which capitalist group shall dominate." America's workers must not allow themselves to be used like their European comrades. They must realize that they "have no country," that "the only flag worth fighting for . . . is the red flag." They must *"declare beyond any shadow of a doubt that they will not make war on any nation for the benefit of the profit-taking class of America!"* Nor should the Socialist Party of America shrink from its responsibilities, as had the German Socialists, whose representatives in the Reichstag had unanimously voted war credits. On the contrary, the party "must meet the issue FACE TO FACE" and "go on record for a General Strike in the time of war."[13]

That the United States proved unable—or unwilling—to resist the war mania, committing itself to the struggle in April 1917, was reason enough for Mary to despair. But she soon had additional reasons for chagrin. Not only were many Socialists and IWW members jailed by the federal government for violating the Conscription Act and, later, for their opposition to the Espionage and Sedition Acts of 1917 and 1918 that together declared practically all antiwar agitation illegal, but the *Review* was one of a number of radical publications—among them the *Appeal to Reason,* the *Milwaukee Leader,* and the *Masses*—which died a death of government-caused attrition. Late in June 1917, the *Review*'s editors were informed that the June issue, which featured on its cover a cartoon depicting a huge pile of human skulls on top of which rested a throne holding a money bag labelled "capitalist interest," was unmailable and that the July issue must be submitted to Washington for aproval. The July number was subsequently also ruled unmailable, in part because its cover portrayed an American solider peering through a store window at a collection of "deformity apparatus," including artificial limbs. The August issue was passed by the Washington censors after three paragraphs to which they objected were deleted, but the *Review*'s staff was unable to mail any copies of the magazine during the six months that followed. Ironically, the September number included Mary Marcy's "A Month of Lawlessness," an article deploring the persecution of opponents of the war. The periodical's last issue was that of February 1918.

After the *Review*'s termination, Mary continued her employment as secretary of Kerr & Company, and Leslie assisted in managing the publishing house's business affairs. Although the change in their status resulted in an unfortunate reduction in the couple's income, it did not idle Mary's pen. Not only did she continue to turn out, in rapid succession, books, pamphlets, leaflets, a "social problem" play satirizing "free love," and articles in such radical periodicals as *One Big Union Monthly*, the *Liberator*, and the *Industrial Pioneer*, but she engaged increasingly in the writing of free verse and corresponded regularly with workers in America, Australia, Japan, and elsewhere. Nor did the end of the *Review* diminish her political activism. In 1918 she joined the IWW, formalizing the impassioned attachment to that revolutionary union that she had developed at least a decade earlier; and, in 1919, when left-wing Socialists deserted their "evolutionist" colleagues and formed the Communist Labor party and the Communist party, Mary played the role of mediator, reminding members of the three factions that each side had its faults and urging them not to let their difference divert them from the common struggle for workers' emancipation.

Yet Mary's last years were troubled ones. Her health gave way; her home was ransacked and many of her personal records seized by the Department of Justice, while her mail and telegrams were intercepted by the United States Army's G–2 "negative" branch, engaged in the surveillance of radicals; many of her friends were in prison for violating the Espionage and Sedition Acts; and, perhaps most upsetting of all, she was ill-used by "Big Bill" Haywood. In the summer of 1919, following Haywood's conviction for activities opposing the war, Mary and Leslie joined Charles Kerr, Clarence Darrow, and William Bross Lloyd—a flamboyant and wealthy Communist who enjoyed driving his expensive car about Chicago with a red flag flying from the back seat—in posting the IWW leader's bail. Because, unlike Darrow and Lloyd, the Marcys' financial resources were meager, they had to put up their modest home on Dearborn Avenue to provide the bail money. Consequently, when Haywood jumped bail and fled to Soviet Russia in 1921, they lost the house. Had Mary lived to read Haywood's autobiography, she would have seen that Leslie's and her kindness were repaid by being ignored. *Bill Haywood's Book* (New York: International Publishers, 1929) contains a single, wholly inconsequential reference to the couple who had been among his most consistent and selfless admirers: "I went to the home of Mary and Leslie Marcy, where I stopped that night."

Mary died in Chicago's Henrotin Hospital on 8 December 1922 of the effects of a dose of paris green taken four days earlier. Although both the *Chicago Evening Post* and the IWW weekly *Industrial Solidarity* kindly printed Leslie's version of his wife's death—that she had mistaken the bright green insecticide for medicine, the truth was different. Homeless and despondent, she had chosen suicide as an alternative to failing health and faded hopes. Her friend and one-time colleague at Kerr & Company, prominent IWW member Ralph Chaplin, who was in jail for antiwar activities at the time of her death, would write of her suicide years later in his autobiography, *Wobbly*: "To her the revolution was a failure. Mary's was an extreme case of that disillusionment from which many radicals were suffering."

On 16 December 1922, the editors of *Industrial Solidarity* paid tribute to their departed comrade as "a woman of marked intellectual ability" and an "able exponent" of the international proletariat. Their judgment contains nothing with which a student of Mary Marcy's career can quarrel. She was indeed an individual whose clear intelligence and skill as a writer made of her an effective proponent of workers' emancipation. But she was still more. She was a person for whom service to "the cause" always took precedence over personal gain, and whose compassion for the oppressed and spirited opposition to economic inequality represented the very best traditions of American radicalism.

Notes

1. From the preamble to the IWW's constitution as quoted in Julian F. Jaffe, *Crusade Against Radicalism: New York During the Red Scare, 1914–1924* (Port Washington, N.Y.: Kennikat Press, 1972), 25.

2. Editorial, *San Diego Tribune*, 4 March 1912.

3. As quoted in Dexter Perkins and Glyndon G. Van Deusen, *The United States of America: A History*, 2 vols. (New York: Macmillan Co., 1962), 2:273.

4. Reprinted in Charles Edward Russell, *The Greatest Trust in the World* (New York: Ridgway-Thayer Co., 1905), 1.

5. Editorial, *International Socialist Review* 11 (July 1910): 46; Mary E. Marcy, "A Straw Man," *International Socialist Review* 13 (March 1913): 691.

6. "The Policy of the Review," *International Socialist Review* 12 (February

1912): 523; "The Socialist Party of America," *International Socialist Review* 12 (April 1912): 679–80.

7. *Socialist Party Weekly Bulletin*, 23 November 1911, as reprinted in Ira Kipnis, *The American Socialist Movement, 1897–1912* (New York: Columbia University Press, 1952), 395.

8. "Verdict—Not Guilty: Report of National Investigating Committee," *International Socialist Review* 12 (June 1912): 864.

9. "A Month of Lawlessness," *International Socialist Review* 18 (September 1917): 157.

10. "Can A Socialist Serve 'All the People'?," *International Socialist Review* 12 (September 1911): 150–51.

11. "We Must Fight it Out," *International Socialist Review* 15 (April 1915):628.

12. "Direct Action," *International Socialist Review* 16 (September 1915):180.

13. "International Capital and the World Trust," *International Socialist Review* 16 (October 1915):241; "The Real Fatherland," *International Socialist Review* 15 (September 1914): 178; "Killed Without Warning By the American Capitalist Class," *International Socialist Review* 17 (March 1917):520; "Socialist Unpreparedness in Germany," *International Socialist Review* 15 (October 1913):246.

1

Exposing the Beef Trust

MARY Marcy published the "Letters of a Pork Packer's Stenographer," excerpts from which appear below, at a time of great controversy over the so-called beef trust. In 1902 three large Chicago meatpackers—Swift, Armour, and Morris—attempted to gain control of the industry by collectively purchasing thirteen other packing companies, which they then formed into the National Packing Company, with Swift owning 47 percent of the stock, Armour 40 percent, and Morris 13 percent. The government promptly attacked these and three additional firms, charging monopolistic practices that had resulted in a large degree of control over the slaughtering and packing of meat. A permanent injunction forbidding the packers to combine was issued by the U.S. Circuit Court in Chicago, but the packers appealed and the case was argued before the U.S. Supreme Court in 1905. Although in *Swift and Company v. United States* (196 U.S. 375) the court for the most part upheld the government's position, it failed to order the dissolution of the National Packing Company, and their monopolistic practices continued. Further attacks on the packers followed the same year and periodically thereafter, but it was only in 1920, after an extensive Federal Trade Commission investigation, that they agreed to dispose of their varied stockyard interests, their retail meat markets, and the wholesaling of lines not directly related to meat packing.

The first installment of Marcy's serial on the packing industry was printed in the *International Socialist Review* of August 1904—just four months after she left her secretarial post with the Armour Company in Kansas City, Missouri—and the final installment appeared in January 1905. The following April she was summoned to appear before a grand jury in Chicago as a witness for the United States government against the beef trust. On the eve of her testimony, officials at Armour and Swift attempted to cast doubt on her credibility as a witness. The *Chicago Tribune* of 26 April reported both C. W. Armour's charge that "If there was anything in our business to hide she did not have access to it," and also the complaint of Swift's manager: "No combination has ever existed among the packers in Kansas City, and this announcement that she knows the secrets of the packers is a dream too vague for even an authoress. It is absurd to give credit to such a sensation as she is trying to make out of nothing."[1] Despite these efforts to discredit her, Marcy's testimony on 28 April was widely regarded as damaging to the packers, particularly her description of how price agreements were arrived at by the companies at special meetings of their representatives each morning and then sent out by code to the firms dealing with them. She explained that one word in Swift's code (a copy of which she gave to the government) might mean "sell all you have left over at a cent under market price today."[2]

The publicity surrounding Marcy's testimony combined with the attention accorded her hard-hitting serial not only set the stage for her subsequent employment on the editorial staff of the *International Socialist Review,* but also gave her some reputation as a "muckraker"—the title given those writers and journalists who in the first decade of the century exposed the less attractive sides of American life. The high point of the muckraking movement was reached in 1905–6 when Upton Sinclair's novel *The Jungle* was published on a theme Marcy included in her "Letters," the Chicago meatpackers' exploitation of workingmen, especially immigrant workers. This most popular and most influential of all Sinclair's novels first appeared serially in the Socialist weekly *Appeal to Reason* and it was then issued in book form by Doubleday, Page and Company, a nonradical publishing house. It sold one-hundred-thousand copies in book form, an extraordinary figure at the time, and its lurid description of the unsanitary conditions under which meat was processed in Chicago slaughterhouses contributed to the passage by Congress in 1906 of both the Meat Inspection Act and the Pure Food and Drug Act.

Notes

1. *Chicago Tribune,* 26 April 1905.
2. Ibid., 29 April 1905.

Excerpts from
"Letters of a Pork Packer's Stenographer"

. . . I am back in dear, dirty old Chicago again—glued to my Remington—as of yore. I returned home just a month ago yesterday, much
stronger and a great deal poorer than I went away. So poor, in fact, that
the day after my arrival, I donned my most business-like frock, and
bought all the morning papers to see what was doing in the stenographic
line. There were the usual half-dozen ads for "Neat and attractive—
experience unnecessary; ten dollar a week" girls, that experience has
taught us to shun, and an enormous demand for the girl who could serve
in every capacity from correspondent to sweep, for $6 a week; but there
was only one position that looked like my sort of a place, and as I knew it
was one of the kind you have to get up early in the morning to secure, I
took the first car out there; met the man who employs the stenographers; was chosen from fifty applicants, and in less than five minutes
was taking dictation from my new "boss," who was reading it off at the
rate of about fifty knots an hour.

But the news that will most surprise you, and delights me, is, that I am
in the employ of the Pork Packer who wrote those famous "Letters to His
Son"!* As I was engaged to be stenographer-in-chief to the General
Manager of the Branch House Department, and have consequently been
able to get a pretty good inside line on the way things are run here, I
want to put you onto a few points from our side of the questions he
wrote about. But none of the things I write, ought to be sufficiently
selfish or vulgar to surprise you, after reading his pages that reeked so
strongly of the sty.

You know I have maintained for a long time that men are largely
products of their environment, and so I am trying to remember that it
would be difficult for a Pork Packer to deal in hogs for forty years
without acquiring some of the characteristics for which they are noted.

I leave at 6:30 in the morning, and generally reach home at the same
hour in the evening, in time for dinner. Twelve hours at the office and
en route don't leave me much strength, nor desire to study the "higher"
things, in the little time I have left for myself. In fact, I am usually so
tired that I prefer my bed to a favorite symphony. . . .

We have thirty minutes at noon for lunch, when all the cattle on the

---

"Letters of a Pork Packer's Stenographer," *International Socialist Review* 5 (August 1904): 102–9; (September 1904): 175–78; (November 1904): 296–303;
(December 1904): 363–69; (January 1905): 418–23.

*John Graham of Graham and Company. Graham and the other individuals
referred to in the following pages are fictitious.

plant and in the office feed. Those in the pens get the best, because the best pays, and we get the cheapest—flap-jacks at 5 cts. apiece, and cold storage No. 3 eggs at 10 cts. each, through the benevolence of the Packing Company, although No. 1s are retailing at 25 cts. per dozen. And they tell us the Graham restaurant is run purely for the convenience of the employees!

Every morning when I come to work, I see a crowd of ragged Austrian, German, Italian, negro, Polish and American workmen in groups before the gates, who, I am told, are always waiting about the plant in the hope of getting a job when an accident occurs, or there is a call for extra men, and as I learn there are often as many as thirty men hurt here in a single day, I suppose the poor fellows do not always have to wait in vain.

The buildings are large, and would be airy, were there any air in this part of the city. They cover many acres, and throng with thousands of working men, and women, and little children every day. We are, in fact, a city in ourselves.

The first day I came down here, I noticed a golden pig that dances airily from a gilded weather vane on the top of the main office, and I am beginning to think it is more significant perhaps, than the historical calf, as an emblem of the spirit of the powers that rule over, and the methods pursued in Packingtown.

I wish you could hear Mr. King (Manager of the Branch House Department) dictate to me. He comes like a whirlwind; begins when he is about ten feet away, and talks like one possessed. He snorts and stews and gives it to the Branch House Managers good and plenty. He never writes unless something has gone wrong, and so his life is one long never-ending complaint; but he glories in it. I wonder every day of my life why the men don't resign. None of their reports are ever so good but that Mr. King growls because they are not better. They always seem to find it necessary to pay higher wages than he wants them to pay, and to sell their goods for a little less than he thinks they ought to get for them. . . .

But to continue with my dictation. There are telegrams galore, and cables to the uttermost parts of the earth, and every few minutes Mr. King goes so fast that his tongue gets twisted, and he runs into a snag. Then he backs up, side tracks, and tears on again regardless of any and every thing, and finally starts away, dictating as he goes. Then I take a long breath and wonder what parts of the mess to transpose.

He treats everybody (except the Grahams) as his natural enemy, though they tell me he says I am one of the only two good stenographers he has had in his thirty-two years experience with the company. If he knew I had heard of it, however, he would fire me tomorrow. I really do try to please him. First, because I need the position; second, because I would rather work for a man who goes like the wind and keeps things moving, than for one whose dictation puts me to sleep; and third, because, better would a mill-stone be tied about my neck, and I be thrown into the lake, than to displease Mr. King. When anything goes wrong, he screams at the top of his voice, and everybody in that end of the office lingers around to be at the killing, and see the fun. In toto he treats us all like dogs. He has driven half the boys to drink, and the girls into nervous prostration. I wondered when the man who engages the stenographers asked if I had "strong nerves" what his object could be; but it did not take me more than ten minutes to find out, after I had met Mr. King. . . .

They tell me Mr King never talks anything but packing-house, even at social entertainments. His shop is his whole house. He talks it on the cars, at lunch, and doubtless, also, he talks it in his sleep. He reminds me of those serfs who died so willingly for their lords in the feudal times, because, while he has worked faithfully for the company so many years, is poor, and old, yet he is prouder than John Graham, himself, because as I have heard him boast, "The sun never sets on the Graham hams and bacon. . . ."

I was here several days before I saw Mr. John Graham (the Pork Packer) himself. The papers said he had been up to Battle Creek two months, for his stomach's sake. When I opened my desk at 7:25 the morning of his return, he was already going over Branch House Reports, ferreting out shrinkages, unnecessary expenses, and questioning any rise in salaries. In less than five minutes he had "fired" one of our Branch House Managers, by wire, for not disposing of some spoiled sweet pickled meats before the health officers got after him, and had dispatched another man to take his place—also by wire. He is indeed a wonderful man in his way. From the time each hog goes into the pen, until it is disposed of to the consumer or dealer, he is able to account for every hair of its hide, and every ounce of flesh and bone (for nothing is wasted here, you know).

He is a rather short, stout, bald, red-faced man, with keen gray eyes that take in discrepancies and shortages at a glance. He knows . . . how to turn tough old canners . . . into . . . canned "Delicatessen Lunch Tongue" . . . ; how to use any old carcass to make "Spring Beauty Toilet Soap"; in short, how to make one dollar in labor produce five dollars in market value. And I would say that John Graham's relation to the production of those four dollars of profit, was just about the same as the relation our "Golden Churn" Butterine bears to the churn! . . .

I have been very busy all morning, writing our Branch House Managers to go through their letter books and destroy any evidences of our "understanding about prices with former competitors." Mr. Graham and Mr. King had a long consultation with Mr. Robinson, the company's chief attorney, which resulted in the following wire, which I dispatched to one of our Branch House Managers at a Southern point:

"Regarding summons reference Beef Trust investigation, have decided will all ignore same. Do not appear."

"*All*," of course, means the five companies in the combination; so you see, there ARE some real American Anarchists—if a rich man ever can be an anarchist. . . .

I wonder if you understand how omnipotent we really are! We represent the only market on which the farmer and stockman can dispose of his product, and on the other hand, we are the only people from whom the Public can buy. Of course, there is nothing monopolistic about this state of affairs. This is a "free" country. If the farmer is not satisfied with our offers, he can ship his poultry and eggs back home. The stockman can do likewise with his cattle, if he asks more than we care to pay. And the dear Public has always the privilege of—doing without.

There is a crazy little man, of the name of Hayden, at Higginsville, Ill., who is running a small butcher shop in competition with our Retail Market there. He doesn't know, of course, that the company he buys his meats of has opened a Parlor Market to compete with him, because it is not known as a Graham shop, but is run under the name of "The People's Market."

Mr. King wrote our Manager at that point to shade his prices a trifle to the consumer, and we have meanwhile raised our prices to Mr. Hayden, and Mr. King says this man ought not last two weeks.

It is only a question of time, Mr. Graham says, until we will completely do away with the middleman. There is no good reason why meat should pass through the hands of three or four men before it reaches the consumers. . . .

It looks sensible on the face of it, to me. It seems as though if a certain amount of the work necessary to present production, and distribution could be eliminated, any intelligent society would want to make use of the means to bring about such a condition. For our object ought to be, not to see how long we can be at work, but to produce enough for everybody, in the least possible time. Of course we understand that in the disorganized state of society today, this would mean still greater production, by fewer men, and greater wealth for the benefit of a few, and that the men who did the work would not be the ones to reap the harvests thereof, because every workingman would be forced to more actively compete with his brothers for the decreasing number of jobs. . . .

Mr. King discharged two of our men today. One of them had been in the employ of the company for twenty-five years, and Mr. Graham said he was "too old." The other was a young cashier, who is "nervous." The moral of the story is, that you must not grow old, nor ill, if you want to hold your job. There is one thing upon which the World of Business is not founded, and that is Sentiment. It is absolutely swallowed up in the clatter of dollars and cents. And I am beginning to believe that the successful business men who are Christians are about as scarce as hens teeth. They may be Baptists, and Methodists, or Catholics, or Scientists, or Seventh Day Adventists, but it is dreadfully hard for them to be Christians. A man may want to be a Christian, but there are his children to be educated, and he decides that he would rather see his competitor's little ones working in a factory than his own, and goes in for a "lawful" or unlawful advantage.

And speaking of factories, reminds me of the manufacturer who launched me on the stenographic sea, and who grew rich hiring children and young girls to run his sewing machines, in manufacturing the dear, old flag, the "Star Spangled Banner," which has come, alas! to mean just that—millions of men, and women and little children, toiling to make money-kings of a few! I might add also that one of the brothers in this company . . . granted public favors, for value received, and said "I done," and "you was," and "fired" me because I told the boys in the office that the "Identity of Interest Between Employer and Employed" fable was all ROT! I argue the question no more, for he proved my assertion.

On the other hand, there was the lumber dealer for whom I worked, who treated every man as though he were his brother; who gave his customers what they purchased, and his employees what they earned, and who—failed! You see many of these men are forced to push their competitors down, in order to avoid sinking themselves; so I am not blaming the individual, but the system. . . .

Today the City gave "us" (for private switching purposes) land valued at $80,000. Verily, verily! as David Harum says, "Them that has, GITS!" . . .

Mr. King has gone down to Savannah to straighten out a sweet-pickled-spoiled-meat-scandal, and so I am helping first in one department, and then in another, wherever a stenographer is ill, or work is heavy; and, while it brings one down to very fine trim, and excellent speed, it is nerve racking, to say the least.

At present I am temporarily installed in the Legal Department; otherwise known among the employees (because of the depravity of their methods) as the "Skin Department." There is also a Hide Department, but we never confuse the two, as their functions are quite dissimilar. In the Hide Department Men skin HOGS, and in the Legal Department, Hogs skin MEN.

I have been here only a few days, and the things I could write on the Legal Department would fill a book. I believe I have learned more on the ways and means of corporation success in this, than I have learned in all the other departments where I have worked.

The Legal Department naturally includes also the Accident Department. In the case of the slightest accident that may happen to an employee, it is the duty of this division to immediately take affidavits from all those present, who witnessed, and who did *not* witness, the accident. They all swear, in order to hold their jobs, to whatever is requested of them; that the machinery was in perfect repair, whether it was nor not, and that the accident was due to the man's own personal carelessness.

I had occasion to write the "statement" of a deaf and dumb man—a "bumper," they called him—who had never laid eyes on the paper until he was called in to sign and swear to it. It is the customary way. The statements are outlined, and the men are always ready to affirm all that is stated therein.

There is always the foreman of the department, who is on the side his salary comes from, and the corporation doctor, ditto; besides the injured man himself, who is usually so badly in need of money that he would sign away his hope in Heaven for ten or twenty dollars in hard cash. Very often the son of the injured man is given a place on the plant, and his daughter a place in the sausage factory, in order to obtain a release on a clear case of liability. The doctor is friendly, and the attorneys kind, unless the claimant shows a disposition to demand justice. And he is given every conceivable method, except a written one, to understand that as long as the Graham plant runs, he will continue in the service of his masters, no matter how disabled he may be. And many of them sign purely on their faith in the security of their future jobs. This, of course, is merely a ruse on the part of the Legal Department, and at the first excuse the disabled man is "laid off."

Last month over four hundred accidents occurred on the Graham plant, and only two of the men injured have brought suit. And I heard the attorneys say it would be a very easy matter to either bluff or force these men to drop them.

It seems that none of the other packers in the combine will give one of them, who is a poultry "picker" and is in urgent need of money, a job. The father of the other man is a retail butcher, to whom the combine has raised its prices, and made strictly C.O.D. terms, and to whom they will, if necessary, absolutely refuse to sell meat. So you see they are not worried over their inability to get these young men into line.

"The Workingmen of America," said Doctor Hughes, in the Sunday paper, "are an extravagant and improvident class." Of course! They should have *saved* their money when they retained all four of their limbs!

One of them received $9.00 a week, and only had four children! I wonder why he didn't lay up a few thousand against a "rainy day!"

Yesterday a despairing workman, who had been injured through the falling of one of the freight elevators, muttered something about a "damage" suit when the attorneys offered him $20.00 as compensation for the loss of his foot. They smiled pityingly upon him and said, "Don't you know, my man, that your case will never come up?" Then they turned their backs upon him, and seemed lost in other matters. And this morning the same workman came in *anxious* to sign the release for the sum that he yesterday scorned.

They tell me there is in Kansas City a judge who has never rendered a decision against a corporation. Think of it—a judge over men, elected by the workingman—and throwing all his influence as well as his decisions for the benefit of the Rich! But of such are the courts.

We received a letter from our————Texas house yesterday, enclosing a "bad debt" for collection, along with a statement of the year's sales, aggregating $2,800,325.89, of which this debt of $102.35 represented the total loss on accounts upon their books. So you see that any money Father Graham *risks* in this business is a very small percentage of one per cent.

When Graham & Company invest one dollar (which covers the price paid to the stockman for cattle, rents, taxes, interest—6 per cent to the banker—labor on the plant and in the offices, the expenses of selling and collecting) they add 50 or 60 per cent as profits, and charge the retail butcher $1.60 for meat costing them one dollar. The dealer, of course, pays the freight—probably 10 cents—which makes his meat cost him $1.70. He then adds 50 percent of his investment (or 85 cents) in selling to the consumer (which must cover shrinkage, rent, assistants, losses— which usually amount to about 15 per cent—and *profits*). The consumer pays then $2.55 for meat that actually *costs* (all profit deducted) only about 60 or 65 cents.

These observations cause one to wonder why the "Legal" rate of interest permitted to banks, should not be applied to interest (or profits made) upon all money invested in business enterprises as well. Surely 50 per cent is robbery! The customer is not getting the worth of his money, nor the employee the value of his labor! . . .

One of the girls left yesterday to get married. She was thirty-two years old, and had worked for the company twelve years. She confessed to us very frankly that she had made up her mind to accept the first man who could offer her a home, and when that man happened to be all she had previously despised, she fixed her thoughts on the joys of a steady income, and decided to marry the business.

All the girls, I am sure, would like to marry. And a great many men also, but there are few of them who earn salaries large enough to support a wife, and so the girls sigh alone, and the young men go to the dogs.

Women do marry—a smaller percentage every year—and generally for a home. And there are occasionally those who put their "Trust in Providence" and start in on $12.00 a week; but they soon learn that Providence does NOT provide, and that existence based upon the things one can live without, is not the best foundation upon which to build a happy home. And now and then there is still a happy, comfortable love match, like the stories of fifty years ago, but the majority are the thousands of Marys waiting for the thousands of Teddies—and the increase in salary that never comes.

. . . I am no different from the rest. But I have seen too many of the "trusting" kind come to grief to care to bring children into the world, to fight the dreadful battle of life, at this uncertain stage of civilization. And I think the man who goes about spouting a "Multiply and replenish the earth" doctrine, as long as men are not certain that their children will have plenty to eat and wear, good health, and an education—a chance for happiness—is a fool! He would better spend his efforts in bringing about a society that would be fit to bring little children up in.

I see by the papers that Old John Graham is trying to lay the blame upon the workingman for the present high prices on beef. Coal, he also says, is 10 cents per bull higher than it was a year ago. This would, you can easily see, make a vast difference in the cost of a 1,000 pound animal. But his principal howl is about the greedy, greedy workingman, who is getting from 5 per cent to 10 per cent more in wages than he was a year ago. But he forgets to tell the papers of the innumerable methods employed to increase the output of the individual workman, until, in most cases, wages have decreased in proportion to the number of cattle they are compelled to handle now compared to the number they prepared two years ago.

Every day some new way is devised to eliminate some portion of the salary account in the various departments in the offices. They tell me that bookkeepers rarely receive more than $50.00 per month—about one-half what they were able to demand fifteen years ago. One of the inspectors came around through all the offices last week and discharged from three to five in every department, merely adding a little extra work to the burdens of the "fortunates" who were retained.

Gradually the Accounting, the Credit and Branch House Departments are being removed from Kansas City and established here in Chicago. W——& Company have already laid off almost their entire force in certain departments in Kansas City, which can be managed just as well from the Chicago offices. And it is being whispered about that Graham & Company will soon incorporate similar proceedings.

All the incapable, the useless and outworn, are being daily discarded by Packingtown, under the new and invincible system of combination which is evolving in the Industrial World to-day.

Mr. Robinson (attorney-in-chief) has just come in accompanied by a gang of workmen who were present at an accident where one of "our stickers" was killed. This makes the third man killed on the plant to-day. . . .

. . . "Our" assistant attorney spent the whole day at the County Hospital with one Peter Piper, a truckman, who was injured while crossing one of the chutes, which was so rickety that it gave way, precipitating him across one of the sheep pens, thirty feet below, and breaking his back. It is the fear of the Legal Department that if Peter shuffles out of this vale of tears without signing a release for the company, his wife or brother may bring suit, as the case is clearly one of liability.

And so Attorney Karles waits at Peter's bedside, ready to greet his conscious gaze with a smile full of brotherly love, and a pencil, with which to have him sign away the only hope of the little Pipers for an education and the "higher life." For compulsory education laws don't do much good for the little boy who has no trousers. The demands of the small stomachs are apt to be considered more imperative than the development of their minds, and School Inspectors eluded that the children may earn clothes for their backs and a shelter over their heads. Poor little Pipers!

We received a call from the wife of the Hon. Phony Bumpkin, Alderman of the ——eenth Ward. About a week ago, it seems, while one of "our" guides escorted Mrs. B. and a friend, by whom she was accompanied, through the various departments explaining the wonders of the plant, a linen dress which she wore was spotted with lard by the bursting of a pipe. The line of "The Maimed, the Halt and the Blind" was waylaid outside the Law Office, in order that we might sympathize in private with Her Ladyship, and our attorney-in-charge assured her deferentially that the check for $50.00 which the company presented to her was only to compensate for the inconvenience to which she had been subjected. She explained that while she did not need it and the gown could be cleaned, she deemed it no more than right, etc., etc., and drove majestically away in her carriage.

She was immediately followed by a young workman, who said he was twenty-eight, but who looked much older. Owing to the absence of gates on one of the freight elevators, his right foot had been smashed and consequently amputated two months ago. Immediately upon his appearance the attorney-in-charge became so busily engaged among his papers that it was some time before he noticed the young man at all. As the moments passed, the poor fellow grew more painfully timid and nervous, and finally, reduced to a pitiable state of subjection, signed a statement releasing the company from liability for the magnificent sum of $10.00.

This much have I learned positively, my dear; if you want to gain anything from a corporation, don't say you NEED it, nor that it is right and just that you should have it; but rather that you have more money than you can use—and then demand it anyway, and in all probability you will get all you ask for—particularly if your father is an alderman or a railway official.

One cannot but observe that the old axiom applying to War has been altered in the minds of men to read "All is fair in business"; nor can one help noting the close relation between the two. After all, business is merely a more refined method of war, whereby men become the masters of their fellowmen, not by physical superiority, but through possession of those things whereon their lives depend. And surely no king is so powerful as he who holds the needs of men!

But as I was saying "our" unspoken motto is "All is fair in business." It is the legitimate (?) occupation of getting something for nothing, and so everything is made for profit, instead of for use, or primarily for profit, and only secondarily for use. Profit, not money, it seems to me, is the root of the evil.

Perhaps you remember reading in the newspapers a few years ago, of the sudden exposure of underground pipes that a Chicago Packing Company had secretly laid and connected with the city mains, in order to obtain their water without paying for it, and in this way robbing the city of thousands of dollars annually. Of course you do not remember that anybody was punished for it! No? Well, neither do I; nor does any one, for nobody was punished. There are a good many more thieves out of jails than there are in them; but they are among our most "esteemed citizens," and none of them ever stopped at stealing a loaf of bread. As an observing writer said a short time ago,

"A man goeth to jail for stealing a loaf of bread,
And to Congress for stealing a Railroad. . . ."

I am not as strong as I was five years ago and I am usually a rag by five o'clock. You know how hard I have struggled ever since I was a little girl, to reach the Heights; how I addressed envelopes during the day, and practiced my music in the evening; made out bills while I studied stenography; hammered my Remington all day, and prepared myself for the university at night, and how I worked my way through two years' study there. And you know, too, that it was because my life has been one long, never-ending effort to progress that I have been able to gain a few rounds—a very little of learning, the world would say. And the price that I have paid is health and strength. . . .

It is not the loss of fortune that constitutes tragedy; not Death, nor the defeat of an army; nor kings overthrown! It is the toiling man and woman, old at twenty-five; the daily death of sweet desires, of natural impulses; of longings crushed; the growing soul, without room for growth; the mechanical effort; the forgetfulness of everything, save work and bread and sleep; and work, and bread, and sleep, until the final curtain falls!

Something is wrong somewhere, dearie! Something is wrong! I cannot tell you what it is; but the ignorance, and poverty, and misery in the world, prove to us that the wrong is there! Show us that there is something better, nobler, happier than the society of to-day, and the society of yesterday. Harmony and happiness crown all efforts made along natural laws, and a society that produces wars, prisons,, poverty and prostitutes, in a land of plenty, is not based upon those laws.

If there is plenty for all, surely the man and woman who toil should have enough! Something is wrong somewhere, dearie; but I am too tired this evening to try to think it out. This much only do I know. They tell us the country is "afflicted with overproduction," and I, who have worked always, have need of many things. . . .

It is not riches I want; nor power; nor yet fame! It is to make work a means, and not the end of living; to have a little play among the toil; to watch the sun rise in the freshness of the morning; to see the spreading of leaves, and the growing of flowers; to progress a little, instead of losing a little; to be able to pause, amid our hurry-ever, to rest and dream awhile!. . .

I wrote a letter for Mr. Ralston this morning to a man who complained at having to pay for fifty pounds of beef, when he only received 42 pounds, saying that when he sold cattle to the Packing Company, he not only had to pay the freight, but was only paid for what the cattle weighed here.

You see, when a farmer ships to this point we pay him the market price (made by us), and when we ship back to his town, or to him, we weigh the meats, and he pays for what we think our weights are—here at the plant. If he refuses, we ship him no more meats—and naturally (or artificially) he goes out of business. . . .

I have also written to fifty or sixty employers this morning, whose names were furnished the company as references, by men applying for jobs. Some of these applications would make your heart ache. There is one from a teamster, aged thirty-five, who wants a place, and who is "willing to work for $6.00 a week"; who has "no other means of support," but who has "a wife and four children." The blanks he was required to fill out covered the history of his life—twenty years of hard work—and small pay. Is it any wonder that the factories are filling up with little children! For even the Poor Man must eat! Or is it any wonder that Poor Men steal! *Six* dollars a week, in a land of "Overproduction"!

We received a letter from our Branch House Manager at Birmingham, Ala., this morning, enclosing a request from the Ladies' Aid Society of the————Church, asking for a donation of two quarts of ice-cream, or some canned goods, for their Sociable, which will take place tomorrow evening. Our Branch House Manager advised the Ladies that he would refer the matter to Kansas City, who were, in turn, compelled to refer it to us. We will reply to our Kansas City Office tomorrow, to write to our Birmingham Manager, to say to the President of the Ladies' Aid Society, that we regret that her request reached us too late to give us an opportunity of being of service to the Ladies. . . .

I note, by your letter, how much you like Prof. Hadley's course on the Trusts, and I have read, with a great deal of interest, your brief review of his viewpoint. And, as far as he goes, I most emphatically agree with him. What IS the use of having ten factories when two will accomplish the necessary work, or a Middle-man, when it is a saving labor to do away with the Middle-man. Combination certainly DOES do away with the useless—useless labor, useless establishments, useless waste, useless everything, save the profit-drawing, useless Sylvias.* Trusts do also regulate the supply. They produce all that is necessary and no more—which is another sensible feature.

But here is where your University Professor stops, and here is just where I go on. He may SEE further, but self-preservation probably dictates that he say nothing to offend the so-called University Benefactors. There was once a University Professor who taught the truth, and offended the man who held the pocketbook; and he lost his job. Perhaps he stands as an example to those who remain.

If, instead of the present form of the private Trust, all the workingmen of the world united to do the necessary work of the world in the best possible manner, in the least possible time, each worker to receive the fruits of his individual effort, I think this form of combination would be beneficial to everybody. It seems to me, that if Justice prevailed in a land of "Over-production," everybody who worked would have enough.

But the Trusts, as they exist to-day, are not formed for the purpose of

---

*Sylvia Graham, "Pork Packer" John Graham's wealthy daughter.

lowering the market price of any commodity, nor for shortening the working hours of labor, or raising the wages of labor. They are formed for the purpose of cutting down the "cost of production"; gaining control of the market, and finally—and entirely—for making larger profits for the benefit of a Few.

And I want to say right here that there is only one item that can possibly enter into the "cost of production," and that this item is Labor. Labor, from the miners, who wrest the treasures from the earth, and gave them value, from the Lumbermen, who fell the trees, from the men who build, run (and do NOT own) the Railroads, on through the factory, where other bands of workers mold the metal, or carve the timber, or dress the cattle, for the use of the World. It is Labor only that produces wealth, and the "cost of production" is the wages paid to labor for the wealth it has produced. The cost of production (wages paid to Labor) plus the profits, equals the market price of a commodity.

Profits are what a man's employees earn, and do not receive; or what his customers purchase, and do not procure. If the employer rendered unto his customers the full value of their money, or unto his employees the full value of their work, he would have no profits, and the world would be minus its millionaire Sylvias.

When a customer pays my employer $5.00 for work that I have done, and for which I have received only $1.00, it is obvious that either the customer is being cheated, or else, I am.

We know very well that the Trusts of to-day, having secured control of the market, make their own prices. And we see the price of all Trust-made commodities going steadily skyward, in spite of the fact that the cost of production has greatly decreased.

Take the Beef Trust for an example. We represent the only market in which the farmer and stockman can dispose of their produce, cattle and hogs. We represent the only market on which the People can buy. A few representatives of the Trust convene every morning to decide upon the market price of the cattle we buy, and the market price of the beef we *sell*. And I only ask you to note, that cattle were never so low, nor beef so high.

We read a lot in the papers about the prosperity of the working-man, about his glorious increase in wages, and his enviable condition all around; but we forget that during the past five years, the cost of living has almost doubled, and that a man's wage is not the amount of money he receives, but what that money will buy. It takes nearly two dollars to-day to buy what one dollar would have bought a few years ago. . . .

It seems to me that combination is only another step in the evolution of society; but I believe that the benefits should be reaped by you and me, and all the workers, as well as Sylvia, or by you and me rather than

Sylvia, because we are useful, while she is merely an ornamental, member of society.

The Packing Company contracted for a new sausage machine to-day, which will enable them to turn off half the men employed in that department. It will—in the usual way—materially lessen the cost of production, but having a monopoly, they will not need to lower their selling prices.

After all, what benefit has Labor ever received from the "labor saving" inventions? I cannot recall a single instance where the full benefit has not been reaped by the drones alone. . . .

. . . The country is ever, by the aid of these new inventions, growing more productive. By and by, I suppose a few over-worked workingmen, with the aid of these machines, will be able to produce enough to supply the whole world, and the condition of the working man and woman will be much worse than it is now, because the total wages paid to them for producing all the wealth of the world will be so low that they will be able to buy back only a very small percentage of their product; and society will be in a constant state of panic.

We boast about our scientific age, and strut about telling of our wonderful machinery, and brag about the productiveness of America, but I wish we could have a chance to be proud because every citizen of America—and every citizen of the world—owned his own home, was sure of his job, and had plenty to eat and wear. The prosperity of a country does not depend upon the goods we export; nor the size of our standing army, nor the millionaires to whom we pay tribute, but upon the wealth that is produced, and the justice with which it is distributed among the workers who have produced it.

In another ten years, I suppose the Packing Company will have overhead chutes from Texas to Chicago, into which steers as tough as cactus roots can be stimulated to march northward by the aid of gently administered electric shocks, being fed on the way by the farmer's latest harvest, so that by the time they have walked to the Packing House, they will be corn-fed, and ready to be killed.

Transportation can be saved on the corn and on the cattle. A man will sit upon the top of the Packing House and watch the process through a telescope, and guide the feeding of nations by the pressing of a button— or, very likely, they will have a little boy, or even a little girl, the younger, the cheaper. Automatic type-writers and accountants will be in use. A man in Georgia will drop a five dollar bill in a slot when he wants a porterhouse steak, which will be shot to him through a compressed air tube from Chicago—and we—where will we be!. . .

I am no longer the little girl who stole from her crib and crept down the stairs one Christmas eve sixteen years ago, with the hope of discovering the St. Nicholas of childish fancy, and nursery lore—to lose—her first illusion. Nor the school-girl, who boasted of her American birth, and worshipped her Sons of War, who honored where honor was not due, and blamed where she should have given praise. Nor a Christian, in a land where men compete with each other for the means of existence, and count it noble. No longer the idealist who believes in appealing to the sentiment—the humanity in man.

I am the woman of twenty-three who has buried her illusions, who has outgrown the shell of her past beliefs, who respects the old, only because it has made possible the new, who has seen sentiment fail, and Christianity stagnate, and who believes the only programme calculated to benefit the man and woman of the future, must be, as it has been in the past, founded upon the never-failing stimuli, of personal benefit—self-interest, as a Christ's teachings of a brotherhood in this world were founded upon a personal reward to be reaped in Heaven; as many manufacturers in the North, forty years ago, became abolitionists, and worked for the freedom of the negroes, in order that Northern manufacturers might be able to compete with the Southern markets; as cannibalism died away, when it became apparent to the ancient tribes that they could better use their enemies by making slaves of, than by eating, them; as society has ever progressed through the constant seeking of every individual for his own personal happiness.

I have come to believe that self-interest, and not self-sacrifice, is the law of progress, for no matter how ideal may be a man's aims, how altruistic his motives, or how loving his soul, he has first to supply the needs of his own body, ere the work moves on.

Until of late, however, in spite of my lagging faith in the truth of the Church, my waning respect for college intellect, and my new conception of Man, I had still belief in the laws and institutions of our country—that they were formed for the purpose of protecting the innocent from the guilty—and stood for justice and equality toward all. But again, I say, I have buried another one of my illusions.

I am awakened more fully every day to the fact that the laws are made nowadays more to protect the guilty from the innocent, than to uphold the virtuous; rather to help the strong to become stronger, and to protect the colossal robber in picking the pockets of the poor. I have been reading the morning paper and the trial of the boodlers in Missouri. I see that the Packing Companies are going to "Legally" combine. So, while they were punished (in Missouri, a paltry fine of $5,000) for combining—in May—they are combining, according to Law—in June.

Trusts buy, where they cannot defy—and it is only the poor man who obeys the laws. . . .

It seems to me that it is mockery to talk of Liberty when half a dozen men own the resources on which the lives of the whole nation depend! And that we are only suffering a new kind of slavery, where our backs and our stomachs scourge us onward, and bid us yield homage to the kings, as did the lash of the master's whip, in the days of old! And the hand that holds the job rules the world!

But in spite of the loss of my old beliefs, I have found one rock of truth amid the new. Human nature is ever the same. It has always been the same, and doubtless it will continue so. And human nature is selfish. It seeketh its own. It is compelled to seek its own in order to live. On this fact, and on this fact alone, must the Future build. On this fact has History built, and it is this great natural law, that will eventually bring greater happiness, greater liberty, greater knowledge, and broader life, to all men. Utopia must come as the Republic came—not founded upon the sands of sentiment, or religion—but upon the natural and eternal law of self-interest. . . .

. . . Doctor Hughes, whom I heard at Church last Sunday evening, says we owe all our pleasures, and even our lives, to the kind and brotherly capitalist. It is just such sermons as this that make me stay at home, or go to the theater on Sunday evening. I never heard a minister preach anything but contentment and endurance with society as it exists to-day, and from all I can learn, it has been their attitude in all time past, and at their present rate of progress, it seems to me this will continue to be their stand in the future. God is always pleased with the existing state of society, and to oppose such a condition would be to oppose the will of God himself, is the teaching we generally hear from the pulpit. It is the reason progressive thinkers go another way. Anything that retards progress should be set aside, and so they *ought* to go another way. But we find that most ministers, like all other men, form their opinions largely at the source from which they draw their salaries (the wealthy parishioners of the diocese).

All these ecclesiastical theories on endurance, and these college philosophies founded on property, are enough to make anybody sad-hearted. It is not charity we want, but justice; not to be told to endure, when there is a cure; nor to render thanks when we have been the givers of gifts; nor to wait for justice in Heaven, amid injustice here! And it isn't a just Government that permits one child to be born a millionaire, and another a pauper!. . .

2

The Soul and the Heart of American Socialism

FEW radicals have had a more profound impact on the people of their generation than Eugene Victor Debs (1855–1926), the soul and the heart of American socialism. An ardent crusader with a burning hatred of all forms of social injustice, he was perhaps the most controversial—yet popular and effective—socialist figure ever to appear in America. The acrimonious English dramatist and critic George Bernard Shaw announced that "the only safe place for an honest man like Debs was the White House"; Clarence Darrow, the famous lawyer, considered him the kindliest, gentlest, most generous man he had ever known; the British-American novelist, critic, and biographer Frank Harris wrote of him as "the man who had more of the spirit of Jesus in him than any man I have ever met"; and on the occasion of his death the *Nation* asserted that he belonged "to the republic of the immortals whose memory is a living inspiration to mankind." In sharp contrast, Justice Oliver Wendell Holmes dismissed Debs as a "noted agitator," the *Chicago Herald* described him as a "reckless, ranting . . . lawbreaker," and Theodore Roosevelt declared that Debs had "done as much to discredit the labor movement as the worst speculative financiers or most unscrupulous employers of labor and debauchers of legislatures" had done "to discredit honest capitalists and fair-dealing businessmen."[1]

There was little in the circumstances of Debs's early life to foretell the unique place he would occupy in the history of American radicalism. He was born in a plain wooden shack in Terre Haute, Indiana. His parents, who had come to American from Colmar, Alsace, were poor, hardworking people. Of ten children, only six reached adult age. Owing to financial hardship, schooling stopped for Eugene at fourteen, and he went to work in the shops of the Terre Haute and Indianapolis Railway, later becoming a locomotive fireman. When a local of the Brotherhood of Locomotive Firemen was organized in Terre Haute in 1875, he took an active part, and a few years later, he became the national secretary and treasurer of the union and the editor of its magazine. Throughout the eighties he not only continued to work for the union, but he also spent several years as city clerk of Terre Haute and served one term as a Democrat in the Indiana legislature.

An opponent of the craft-union philosophy, in 1893 Debs took part in the formation of the American Railway Union, which was open to all workers regardless of their particular jobs. With Debs as its president, in April 1894 the new union gained nationwide prominence in a successful strike against the Northern Pacific Railroad. Two months later, when employees of the Pullman Company at South Chicago went on strike, the American Railway Union agreed to aid them by refusing to move Pullman cars. Although Debs had initially opposed the action as inexpedient, once the decision was made, he bent every effort to support the strike. And he paid dearly for his trouble. Concurrent with the arrival of federal troops sent by President Cleveland to maintain order and prevent interference with the delivery of the mail, the federal court in Chicago issued a sweeping injunction against the strikers, and in February 1895, Debs was sentenced to six months in the McHenry County jail at Woodstock, Illinois. According to his own word, he spent much of his time while in prison reading the works of Karl Marx and the works of the English socialist Robert Blatchford, as a consequence of which he came to regard the Pullman episode as a practical lesson in the class struggle.

In 1897, the year that he announced his conversion to socialism, Debs transformed what was left of the American Railway Union into a colonization group known as the Social Democracy of America. Three years later he was among those Social Democracy members who joined with representatives of other radical organizations and reform groups to put together what formally emerged in July 1901 as the Socialist Party of America. As his party's candidate for president in 1900, 1904, 1908, and 1912, Debs gained national attention. In 1900, despite the fact that the party was still incomplete, he received 94,768 votes. In 1912 he polled almost 900,000 votes, nearly six percent of the total—a percentage never again equaled by a Socialist candidate.

It was under Debs's leadership that the party enjoyed its greatest national popularity. Although he was at no time the organization's intellectual leader—a role that demanded a more skilled theoretician—he was clearly its spiritual leader, its great moral force. Debs seemed to feel genuinely the empathy with the downtrodden and exploited that other men only talked about. While he lacked the hardheadedness of the politician and he often stood aside, not participating in party discussions or attending party conventions, he was unrivaled in his ability to communicate the urgency of the class struggle and the socialist vision of a future society liberated from capitalism.

When World War I broke out, Debs branded it as a conflict between two groups of capitalists in which the proletariat of each side had nothing to win and much to lose. Although he did not attend the Socialist party's emergency national convention in St. Louis in 1917, he staunchly supported its antiwar proclamation. At the Socialist state convention in Canton, Ohio, in June 1918 he bitterly denounced the Wilson administration's persecution of war protestors. As a result of his remarks he was indicted for violating the Sedition Act, which made it a crime to express antiwar sentiments to an audience that included men of draft age, and was tried in Cleveland, Ohio, in September 1918. The verdict of guilty and the ten-year prison sentence were subsequently upheld by the Supreme Court and Debs entered prison in April 1919. In the following year, while still incarcerated in the federal penitentiary at Atlanta, Georgia, he was nominated for the fifth time as his party's candidate for president. Although the Republican standard-bearer, Warren G. Harding, won one of the most sweeping victories in American politics, Debs did surprisingly well, polling roughly 3.5 percent of the total vote. On Christmas Day 1921, he was released by presidential order, after having served thirty-two months of his sentence. He was not pardoned, however, and consequently his citizenship was not restored.

Mary Marcy's admiration for Debs is clearly revealed in the short essay reprinted below, which she wrote in the summer of 1910 as an introduction to a collection of his writings and speeches. The essay is followed by the letter Debs sent Mary's husband upon learning of her death in December 1922.

Note

1. Ruth Le Prade, ed., *Debs and the Poets* (Pasadena: Upton Sinclair, 1920), 6; Herbert M.Morais and William Kahn, *Gene Debs* (New York: International Publishers, 1948), 10; Frank Harris *Latest Contemporary Portraits* (New York: Macaulay, 1927), 103–4; "Eugene Victor Debs," *Nation* 123 (3 November 1926): 443; Max Lerner, *The Mind and Faith of Justice Holmes* (Boston: Little, Brown, 1943), 442; *Outlook* 127 (11 May 1921): 49.

A Tribute to Debs

Socialists are not hero-worshippers. We do not believe that occasionally great men have been created who have lifted the human race a notch higher or a degree forwarder. Neither do we put our faith in leaders.

We understand that the emancipation of the working class will not be granted by the generosity of the capitalist class, nor by the acumen and honesty of great leaders. Wage workers must trust in themselves. Their interests alone are at all times identical.

We KNOW that socialism is INEVITABLE because men seek pleasure, because they may be counted upon to turn toward ends that promise welfare and happiness to themselves.

We realize that men who lift themselves out of the ranks of the workers are no longer on the same plane as the workers. Only people in the same economic position see things alike and feel the same needs.

It is only natural that leaders should desire to continue to lead. An author believes he is able to teach, and a teacher thinks he is wiser than his pupils. So the men who arise out of the labor movement believe they are chosen to direct and guide those still engaged in the conflict. They are likely to return to their belief in the Great Man Theory, since they have become "great men." Also they are more than likely to become conservative when they have something to lose.

The revolutionary impulse bubbles up always from beneath. "Leaders" regulate their conduct in accordance with what they count their best interests, or happiness. Men who have positions to lose become timid. They are forever cautioning the workers not to move too swiftly. They wish to be perfectly sure of not losing private prestige and advantages in the wonderful-days-a-coming-for-all-the-workers. Often they lose faith in the revolution itself.

Leaders will never be able to carry the workers into the Promised Land. Men do not wage the great Class Struggle in the study nor in the editorial rooms. Methods of class warfare do not come from the brains of the isolated scholar, but from the brains and experiences of the fighters. The workers are the fighters and the thinkers of the revolutionary movement.

Partly for this reason we write a book about our Eugene V. Debs. He is one of the workers; one of the thinkers; one of the fighters.

In the usual sense, he has never been a leader of workingmen. He has never been a guide to the Labor Movement. But, by choice of it, joy in it,

---

Introduction to *Debs: His Life, Writings and Speeches*, 3d ed. (Chicago: Charles H. Kerr & Co., 1910), v–vii.

love of it, he remained a part of the movement itself. Separate him from the revolutionary working class movement and you lose Eugene V. Debs. He is bone of its bone; flesh of its flesh. His life, his hopes and aims are interwoven into the very mesh of the labor movement.

Foolishly we have sometimes asked Debs to lead us; but we have found him ready only to serve. No inducement in the world is great enough to win him from the ranks of the revolution, because he finds his greatest joy in fighting in THE RANKS of the revolutionary army. He has LOST HIMSELF IN HIS CLASS.

The old morals taught us so long by the masters of present day society have ceased to appeal to the working class. Class societies produce class moralities. Those who own the means of life to-day are still teaching us to be "honest," for honesty protects private property; to be "industrious," and produce greater profits for them; to "save for a rainy day," and lower the tax charity imposes upon the rich; to "live cheaply," and lower WAGES and the standard of living. All these virtues reflect the interests of the capitalist class.

But in the storm and stress of things, it would be strange if we workers did not evolve a code of ethics in our own behalf, a line of conduct which we count praiseworthy. This new morality we call CLASS CONSCIOUSNESS.

To workingmen and women this is the greatest of all virtues; and this is the virtue possessed transcendently by Eugene V. Debs. He is a living, loving monument of class consciousness.

For we offered to make him a leader over men. And in this there is much joy and comfort and ease and adulation. And there is love too, perhaps, without understanding.

But Debs refused these things. He does not want to climb up, or to go ahead to lead us. He remains in the ranks and works beside us, slowly, laboriously, patiently, joyously. And this is the only way in which men can help us, for from the ranks come the workable methods of fighting the enemy—born of the needs and requirements of the working class.

If you were to ask Eugene V. Debs if he expected ever to find new interests, to work in new fields of activity or to engage in any other Cause, he would doubtless reply, with that whimsical smile playing about his mouth:

"There isn't any other Cause."

This is the spirit that shall bring the working class to victory. It is the flame that has illumined the life of Eugene V. Debs. Always has he been willing to put away dearly loved friends and dearly loved things for his Best Beloved, the interests of his CLASS.

A Tribute Returned

Terre Haute, Ind., December 16th, 1922

My Dear Leslie Marcy:

Your message containing the very sad, heart-breaking news has just come into my hands. How deeply pained and cruelly shocked I feel to hear of your dear Mary's going out cannot be expressed on this cold sheet of paper.

What a thousand pities this noble heart should have ceased to beat and this brilliant mind to think in the very morning of life! It is impossible for me to realize what you say and my heart refuses to believe that Mary Marcy is dead. I did not see her often, but I knew her well, and I loved and honored her more than well. She was one of the clearest minds and greatest souls in all our movement, and her passing into the great silence will be such a loss as will leave an aching void to those who knew her, for her place can never be filled. I admired her for her uncompromising integrity, and I loved her for her high-souled devotion to her ideals and her personal loyalty to her comrades. She was a sweet, fine, brilliant and truly noble little woman, and her precious memory will be sacredly cherished by me to the last of my life.

The book of Mary's, her last contribution to the cause, has just come and is in my hands, and I am thanking her and you through my tears. It is a rare volume and one we shall treasure among our garnered riches and most precious possessions.*

Leslie, dear comrade, our hearts are with you and we share your bereavement as her soul goes marching on and grows more radiant with the passing years.

With love and sympathy and tears,

Yours always,

EUGENE V. DEBS.

Debs's letter is reprinted from Jack Carney, *Mary Marcy* (Chicago: Charles H. Kerr & Co., 1922), 15.

*Debs is referring to Mary Marcy's *Rhymes of Early Jungle Folk* (Chicago: Charles H. Kerr & Co., 1922).

3

Lessons on Marxian Economics

BETWEEN November 1910 and July of the following year, the *International Socialist Review* featured an eight-part series of "lessons" penned by Mary Marcy in response to numerous requests from subscribers for a course in Marxian economics. Written in simple, direct prose, and accompanied by "Study Questions," the lessons were, in Marcy's words, "an attempt to say, in the language of working men and women, the things Marx says in his own books." Reminding her readers that "Socialism depends for its strength upon the intelligence of its membership, every one of whom is an active educator for the revolutionary movement," she urged them to use the lessons as no more than an introduction, and to purchase and study *The Communist Manifesto*, Marx's *Value, Price and Profit*, and Friedrich Engels's *Socialism: Utopian and Scientific*.[1]

The lessons attracted so favorable a response that in 1911 they were published in a fifty-eight-page pamphlet entitled *Shop Talks on Economics*. The opinion of a Louisville, Kentucky, socialist that Marcy had devised "one of the greatest methods of education that has ever yet been published for educating and training members of the Socialist Party in the science of Marxian Socialism"[2] was widely shared. Eugene Debs, for example, declared:

> Mary E. Marcy's *Shop Talks on Economics* ought to be put in the hands of every wage-worker. Marx is here introduced to the worker in terms he can readily understand and Socialism is made so plain than he cannot escape it. Mrs. Marcy has a peculiar facility for this kind of work and in preparing this most excellent primer on economics for the education of the workers she has rendered an invaluable service to the working class.[3]

Still more indicative of the pamphlet's appeal, by the time of its author's death at the end of 1922, *Shop Talks on Economics* had been printed in seven foreign languages, including Chinese, and over two million copies had been sold throughout the world.

The first four selections that follow are reprinted from Marcy's eight-part series in the *International Socialist Review.* They appeared as the first, second, fourth, and eighth chapters of *Shop Talks on Economics.* The concluding selection is from "Marxian Economics," a series of *Review* articles written by Marcy in 1917. Intended as a supplement to the earlier lessons, the articles concentrated, in particular, on the position of transportation workers and farmers.

Notes

1. Prefatory note to "Beginners' Course in Socialism and the Economics of Karl Marx," *International Socialist Review* 11 (November 1910): 281.
2. "News and Views," *International Socialist Review* 14 (February 1914): 504.
3. *International Socialist Review* 12 (November 1911): inside front cover.

What You Sell to the Boss

If you are a workingman or woman, no matter what you do in a shop or factory or mine, you know that there are TWO kinds of power used in the plant—human, or LABOR-POWER, and steam, or water (or perhaps—gas—explosion) power.

The owner of a new barrel mill in Indiana decided it would be cheaper to have some company furnish POWER to run his mill than to install a power plant himself, so he sent for the three representatives of the three power plants in that city.

The first man came from the company that offered to run the machines in the mill by STEAM power; the second came from a firm which wanted to sell him a gasoline engine to furnish power by the explosions of gas, while the third came from a great water-power company. This man offered to supply power to run the mill machinery at a lower price than the others asked. Of course, he secured the contract.

By this time the mill owner was almost ready to have his plant opened. He had logs (or raw material) ready to start on; he had machinery and power to run that machinery. Only one thing more was needed to start the plant running and to produce staves and hoops for barrels. This was the COMMODITY which you workers supply. It is HUMAN POWER, human LABOR-POWER.

One hundred years ago almost everything was produced by human labor-power, but gradually improved machinery has been invented that lessens the human toil needed to make things. Big machines, run by steam, or water-power, now do most of the heavy and difficult work. But the owner of the mine or factory or mill needs one other COMMODITY to guide the machines, to prepare raw material for the machines, to tend the machines and feed them. He needs YOUR LABOR-POWER.

The barrel manufacturer in Indiana said he needed "hands." He meant HANDS TO DO things. He meant LABOR-POWER. So he put an advertisement in the paper reading "Men Wanted." Of course he did not want to buy MEN outright, as folks used to buy chattel slaves. He hired some of you to work for him. He bought your human POWER (to work)—your LABOR-POWER.

And you sold him your LABOR-POWER, just as a stockman sells horses or a baker sells bread. You went to the boss with something to SELL. He was in the market to BUY human LABOR-POWER, and if your price was low you probably got a job.

Some of us work many years before we realize that even we wage-

"Beginners' Course in Socialism and the Economics of Karl Marx," *International Socialist Review* 11 (November 1910): 281–82; (December 1910): 334–35; (February 1911): 483–85; (July 1911): 37–38.

workers have ONE COMMODITY to sell. As long as we are able to work we try to find a BUYER of our LABOR-POWER. We hunt for a job and the boss that goes with a job. . . .

High prices for LABOR-POWER is what wage-workers want. LOW prices for LABOR-POWER is what your employer wants. . . .

The Value of a Commodity

. . . Now ALL commodities are the product of labor, that is, there was never a commodity that was not the result of the strength and brains of workingmen or women. Workers make shoes; bakers of bread are workingmen or women; houses, street cars, trains, palaces, bridges, stoves— all are the product of the laboring man. ALL commodities are the product of labor.

There is one common thing which all commodities contain. This is LABOR. A commodity only has value (exchange value) because it contains human LABOR.

Horses are commodities; cows are commodities; gold is a commodity. HUMAN LABOR has been spent on producing all these. Labor-power is also a commodity, the result of human labor in the past.

Workingmen and women spent LABOR producing you and me. Somebody made bread, sewed shoes, built houses and made clothes *for us*. All the things we ate and drank and wore and used were made by the labor of workingmen and women. Their labor was NECESSARY labor. Without it we should never have grown old enough or strong enough to have LABOR-POWER to sell. Labor was spent in RAISING us to the point where we would be able to work.

The value of a commodity is determined by the social labor-time necessary to produce it. . . . [As] Marx says:

> It might seem that if the value of a commodity is determined by the quantity of labor bestowed upon its production, the lazier a man, or clumsier a man, the more valuable his commodity, because the greater the time of labor required for finishing the commodity. This, however, would be a sad mistake. You will recollect that I used the word SOCIAL labor, and many points are involved in this qualification.
>
> In saying that the value of a commodity is determined by the quantity of labor worked up or crystalized in it, we mean the quantity of labor necessary for its production in a given state of society, under certain social average conditions of production, with a given social average intensity, and average skill of the labor employed.

If you spend three months cutting up a log with an pen-knife into a kitchen chair, it will be no more valuable in the end than the kitchen chair made in the big factories where many men working at large machines produce hundreds of chairs in a single day.

Of course, we know that every new improvement in machinery lessens the labor-time needed in making certain commodities. Oil is less valuable than it was ten years ago because it takes less labor-power to produce it. Steel has fallen in value, because owing to the new and improved machinery used in making steel it requires LESS human labor-power for its production.

Suppose every shoe factory in the country were working full time in order to supply the demand for shoes. The factories using the very old fashioned machinery would require more labor to the shoe than the factories using newer machines, while the great, up-to-date factories using the most modern machines would need comparatively little HUMAN labor-power in producing shoes.

The value of shoes would be determined by the AVERAGE (or social) labor-time necessary to make them, or the socially necessary labor contained in all the shoes. . . .

In the same way we may determine the value of laboring-power. Like every other commodity its value is determined by the quantity (or time) of labor necessary to produce it. [As Marx says:]

> The laboring-power of a man exists only in his living individuality. A certain mass of necessaries must be consumed by a man to grow up and maintain his life. But the man, like the machine will wear out, and must be replaced by another man. Besides the mass of necessaries required for his own maintenance, he wants another amount of necessaries to bring up a certain quota of children that are to replace him on the labor market and to perpetuate the race of laborers. It will be seen that the value of laboring-power is determined by the value of the necessaries required to produce, develop, maintain and perpetuate the laboring-power.

The value of man's labor-power is determined by the social labor necessary to produce it, Marx says. This means food, clothing, shelter (the necessities of life) and it means a little more than this. It means something additional to rear a boy or girl to take your place in the shop or factory when you grow too old to keep up the fierce pace set by the boss.

Enough to live on and to raise workers to take our places—this is the value of our labor-power, if we are wage-workers.

How Profits Are Made

Many of us have been accustomed to think that profits are made from graft, from special privileges, or from monopoly. We have talked so much of the thieving among capitalists that we have altogether over-looked the great, main method of profit taking.

As Marx says, if you cannot explain profits on the supposition that commodities exchange at their values, you cannot explain them at all.

And so we shall assume (as in truth they generally do) that com-modities, on the average, exchange at their value.

Suppose that it takes two hours of necessary labor to produce the necessaries of life for a workingman—or, in other words, two hours of labor a day to produce LABORING-POWER.

Suppose too (as is very likely the case), that $2.00 in gold represents two hours of labor.

Now the value of labor-power (which the workingman sells) is deter-mined (as the value of all commodities are determined), by the social labor contained in it. It is represented by the necessities of life, produced by two hours of necessary labor a day.

If the workman sells his labor-power at its VALUE, he will receive in return a commodity containing two hours of necessary social labor. In the case we mention above, he would receive $2.00 a day.

In other words, a day's labor-power represents two hours of labor, embodied in the food, clothing and shelter that produce it, just as the two dollars in gold (or an equivalent) represent two hours of necessary labor. The labor-power is equal in value to the value of the $2.00 in gold. The workman has sold his labor-power at its value.

The workman receives enough ($2.00) in wages to eat, drink, to rest and clothe himself—enough to PRODUCE MORE labor-power. He receives the value of his labor-power.

But wage laborers sell their laboring-power to the bosses by the day or by the week, at so many hours a day. The capitalist buys the commodity (labor-power), paying for it at its value. If the wage-worker is a miner, in TWO HOURS he will dig coal equal in value to his wage of $2.00 a day. The coal he digs will contain two hours of labor just as the two dollars in gold contain two hours of labor and as the necessaries for which he exchanges his two dollars, contain two hours of labor.

In other words, in two hours (of necessary labor) the miner would have produced value in coal equal to the value of his wages (or his laboring-power). But he sells his labor-power by the day or week and the boss prolongs the hours of work as far as possible.

In two hours, however, the miner has produced enough value to pay his own wages, but the boss, having bought the laboring-power by the day, may be able to make the wage-worker work ten hours daily. The miner needs only to work two hours to produce a value of $2.00 to reproduce his labor-power. As Marx would say:

He must daily reproduce a value of $2.00 (which he will do in two hours), to daily reproduce his labor-power.

But when he sells his laboring-power to the boss the boss acquires the right to use his labor-power the entire day—as many hours as the worker's physical endurance or fighting resistance will permit.

If he forces the miner to work ten hours daily, the workingman will be laboring EIGHT hours beyond the time necessary to pay his own wages (or value of his labor-power). These eight hours of surplus labor are embodied in a surplus value or a surplus product.

In two hours the miner produces in coal value sufficient to pay for his labor-power, but in the eight succeeding hours of labor, he will produce coal valuing $8.00, all of which the capitalist retains for himself.

Since the miner sold his laboring-power to the capitalist, the coal, or value the miner produces, belongs to the capitalist.

Thus the capitalist spends $2.00 a day in wages (or two hours of labor) and acquires coal, or other commodities, equal to $10.00 (or ten hours of labor). Thus come profits.

Year after year, the capitalists buy labor-power, paying for it at its value (in the case of the miner at $2.00 a day). The capitalists *own* the products of the workers—equalling ten hours of labor. They exchange a commodity (gold, or money), containing two hours of labor for labor-power (containing two hours of necessary labor—and represented by the necessities of life). But when the miner goes home at night the capitalists find themselves OWNERS of the coal he has dug, which contains TEN HOURS OF LABOR.

Coal (representing ten hours of labor) will exchange for gold (or money) containing ten hours of labor; in this case for $10.00.. The miner has produced $10.00 worth of coal. He received $2.00.

The eight hours of value, or $8.00 worth of coal, which the capitalists appropriate, is *surplus value,* for which they give no equivalent. . . .

But intelligent workmen and women are not content with selling their laboring-power at its value. They are coming more and more to demand the value of the PRODUCTS. We are growing weary of being mere commodities, compelled to sell ourselves, for wages at the regular "market price." We are weary of receiving a product of two hours of labor for products containing ten hours of our labor. We are tired of living on meagre wages while we pile up millions for the capitalist class.

This is the chief demand of socialism; that workingmen and women cease selling themselves, or their strength, as commodities. We propose to OWN the commodities we produce OURSELVES and to exchange commodities containing a certain quantity of necessary social labor, for other commodities representing an equal quantity of necessary social labor.

You and I work for the boss because *he* OWNS the factory or mine or railroad or the mill. OWNERSHIP of the means of production and distribution (the factories, land, mines, mills—the MACHINERY that produces things) makes masters of capitalists and wage-workers of you and me.

Socialists propose the ownership, in common, of the mines, mills, factories, of all the productive industries, by the workers of the world.

When you and I and our comrades own the factory in which we work, we will no longer need to turn over to anybody the commodities we have produced. We shall be joint owners of the things we have made socially. We shall demand labor for labor in the exchange of commodities. This is the kernel of socialism. It proposes to make men and women of us instead of COMMODITIES to be bought and sold upon the cheapest market as men buy shoes or cows.

Shorter Hours of Labor

. . . It is true that the working class, as a CLASS, has never been sufficiently well organized to demand a universally higher price for its labor power—a larger portion of the value of its product from the capitalist class.

It is equally true that when they shall have become sufficiently organized and class conscious to do so, they will not stop with asking higher wages, but will abolish the whole wage system itself.

But Capital makes continual war upon the workers. It reduces wages to the bare cost of living and lowers the standard of living whenever and wherever possible. It prolongs the hours of labor as far as the physical endurance of the workers will allow. And the workers find themselves forced constantly to fight in order to hold the little they already have. So that, on every side, we see groups of workers in conflict with their employers, fighting to maintain working conditions, or to improve them where they become unendurable.

It is obvious that men or women working from ten to sixteen hours daily will have little strength or leisure to study, or activity in revolutionary work. It is also patent that wages are bound to be higher where men toil eight hours a day than where they work sixteen hours. It requires two shifts of men, working eight hours daily, to run a machine that one man runs sixteen hours.

It is not only necessary, but it is a highly desirable matter that we continue to resist and to advance and attack in our daily struggles with the capitalists. For it is through present defeats and victories that we learn our strength and our weaknesses. We learn to fight BY FIGHTING. New tactics are often evolved in struggles that seem to be total failures. And class solidarity becomes a living thing, a resistless weapon, when we are fighting and acting more and more as a class. . . .

We must organize along industrial lines to shorten the hours of labor. If an eight hour day were inaugurated, it would mean the additional employment of millions of men and women in America tomorrow. It would insure us leisure for study and recreation—for work in the Army of the Revolution, and it would mean higher wages in America generally. For the fewer men there are competing for jobs, the higher the wage they are able to demand. . . .

Flood the nations with your ballots, workingmen and women of the world. Elect your shop mates, your companions of the mines, your mill hand friends, to every possible office. Put yourselves or your co-workers into every governmental position as fast as possible to render YOUR court decisions, to hold in readiness YOUR army; to control YOUR arsenals and to protect you with YOUR constabulary, to make YOUR laws and to serve YOUR interests and the interests of your fellow workers, whenever and wherever and HOWEVER possible.

AND ORGANIZE INDUSTRIALLY. With YOUR government at your backs, ready to ward off Capitalism, ready at all times to throw itself into battle for you, you can gather the workers of the world into your industrial organization and sign the death warrant of Wage Slavery!

How the Farmer Is Exploited

. . . Because we have been students of only a portion of the writings of Marx, some of us have claimed that the man who owned a farm and worked it himself and sold his product to some warehouse company, or to some speculator, sold his commodities at their value and was, therefore, not exploited in any way. But we were wrong.

As a rule, said Marx, commodities on the average exchange at their value. But by this he did not, by any means, mean that when a farmer sells a thousand bushels of wheat to one man, who in turn sells to a customer, who re-sells to someone else, who finally sells out to a third or fourth buyer—Marx did not mean that all these perfectly useless individuals *added any value to that wheat*. But they sell at a profit.

Now since these speculating purchasers have not added any value to the farmer's wheat, either the first purchaser bought the wheat from the farmer BELOW its value or the final purchaser paid for it at MORE than its value.

The man who originally bought the wheat from the farmer added no value to the wheat nor did his customer, nor his customer's customer,

"Marxian Economics: How the Farmer is Exploited," *International Socialist Review* 17 (April 1917): 621–23.

etc., add any value to the wheat. But the wheat may have sold finally at fifty cents a bushel more than the original purchaser paid for it, because when it was finally sold there was a greater demand for wheat. On the other hand, wheat occasionally sells below the price paid to the farmer for it, because of the sudden termination of war, etc., or by a decrease in the demand for wheat. Supply and demand, we know, affect price, but not value, so that in war time, for example, the farmer may receive a price that is more than the value of his product.

Marx explains in Capital, that brokers, middlemen and merchant capitalists, etc., being, on the whole, unnecessary, produce neither commodities nor any value.

On the average, he says, commodities exchange at their value—that is, the consumer usually buys commodities at their value. He nearly always receives the value he pays for; he gives gold, or its equivalent, representing so many hours of necessary social labor, in exchange for commodities representing an equal amount of necessary social labor.

Commodities usually sell to the consumer at their value. Wheat brokers and wheat and other grain speculators get their profits out of value either produced by the farmer who works his farm, or from value produced by farm tenants or farm laborers, because these products are sold to these speculators BELOW their VALUE.

One speculator buys corn from a group of farmers at 40 cents and re-sells it to another speculator at 46 cents, who disposes of it to a third at 50 cents, who finally sells it to the mill men (who use it as raw material from which, say, corn flakes are manufactured) at 55 cents.

On the average these mill men buy the corn at its value; the various speculators have never seen the corn, never moved the corn, added not one particle of value to the corn. The first speculator in this case bought the corn from the producing farmers at something like 15 cents a bushel BELOW its value. This 15 cents of which the producing farmers were exploited, is divided among the three speculators. Nobody is robbed or exploited but the actual producers of the corn.

Among the capitalist farmers the same conditions prevail as in other fields of investment. Unless the capitalist is able to make his capital bring him the average rate of profits, he seeks other fields in which to put his money.

Capitalist farmers hire farm superintendents, overseers, farm laborers to work their lands or let their farms to farm tenants at a cash rental or for a portion of the tenants' products. Like the capitalist who, for instance, invests his money in a packing house, a mine or a woolen mill, these capitalist farmers have to divide the value appropriated from the labor of the workers with the MIDDLEMAN. The capitalist farmer pays his workers the value of their labor power, but far less than the value of their products. On the average, these products are sold to the final buyer at their value. The capitalist farmer divides the surplus value, produced by the farm tenants or laborers, with the broker, the speculator, the storage companies.

The small farm owner, who works in the fields beside his hired "hands" is an exploiting capitalist as far as he pays his workers wages and appropriates their products. The surplus value or profits he is able to extract are represented by the difference between what he pays for the labor and cost of machinery, maintenance, repairs, taxes, etc., and the price he gets for the products of his laborers. . . .

Socialists are not in the least concerned with helping the . . . town farmer who hires two or three men who run his farm by the aid of additional men in harvest time.This small town farmer also sells the product of the farm workers BELOW its value. We do not grieve to see the expropriator expropriated—the robber robbed. We are concerned only with seeing to it that the working class receives the value of its products. . . .

The small farmer not only pays interest every year on farm loans or rent on farm lands, but, because he has no capital wherewith to buy modern machinery, gets less and less for his labor, because every year a bushel of wheat, a bushel of corn represent LESS NECESSARY HUMAN LABOR than they did before. In other words, wheat and corn and other farm products are steadily decreasing in value because of growing modern machine methods in farm production. . . .

The farmer who owns or is paying on a small farm, who works his farm himself, ought to be interested in the revolutionary movement. He exploits no one and sells his products below their value. . . .

4

The Promise of Socialism

THE four selections that follow demonstrate especially well the strength of Marcy's socialist convictions and her ability to communicate the socialist message in a lively and easily understood manner. They were written when the Socialist Party of America was a vigorous force in the nation's politics and had a profound influence on the reforms and reformers of the day. By 1912 the party's membership had reached an all-time peak of nearly 118,000, making it over five times larger than the largest British socialist party. Eugene Debs attracted almost 900,000 votes in the presidential campaign of that year, while some 1,200 comrades were elected to public office, including seventy-nine mayors. Socialists constituted a significant minority within the American Federation of Labor; they controlled, or were strong in, the Jewish garment unions and such other important unions as the Brewery Workers, the Machinists, and the Western Federation of Miners; and at least the left wing of the Socialist party had a seemingly vital working-class ally in the IWW. Chapters of the Intercollegiate Socialist Society existed on seventy campuses. The Socialist *Appeal to Reason* was one of the world's most popular weeklies, and more than two million readers devoured over three hundred similar newspapers and magazines. Capitalist politicians regarded the Socialists' gains with apprehension, while Socialist party leaders wrote and spoke confidently of eventual victory. Although the party's membership declined drastically following the recall of William D. "Big Bill" Haywood—the titular leader of the left wing—from his post on the national executive committee in 1913, it retained much of its basic strength and character until 1919.

Working Men and Women

We are only working mules, my friend. All over the whole world we are toiling and sweating to make the wheels go around.

We build mansions and palaces and we live in garrets and basements. We sow the fields and reap the harvests—for somebody else to enjoy. We feed the world; we clothe the world; we house the world—and if we are out of a job for one week—we are broke, we are hunting for another master—another boss again.

When we grow so weak and tired and desperate with struggling continually that we are impelled to throw down the whole burden of our lives and pull society about our ears, the Reformers, with loud voices appear.

These Reformers promise us many things. Sometimes they come beneath a Republican banner and again in the Democratic band-wagon. The flag of any movement or organization, dear to you and me, they will float in order to get us to join their ranks.

O yes, they promise many things. Some of these they do not intend to give us; and all they may grant will only render them more secure in their position upon our backs.

Do you remember our philanthropic friend, the New York millionaire, who bought up the land immediately adjoining a great factory and build model tenements for us? Do you remember the rents he charged us were only half as high as the rents we had been paying?

And you remember what happened then? The men who had been laid off offered to take our jobs at lower wages BECAUSE THEY KNEW THEY could LIVE ON LESS, since the RENTS had been reduced. And the boss told us if we refused to accept a reduction in wages, he would have to give our jobs to these men.

So the cheap rents did not help us at all. But they DID HELP the BOSS who was able to cut wages because the cost of living had been lowered.

That is the way reforms turn out. They look like something good for the workers but they always end by benefitting the capitalists.

Low rents, Cheap food, 3 cent car fares—all these the Reformers offer us. But when WE GET them, the COMPETITION for JOBS between the wageworkers themselves brings wages down low enough to take away all we think we have gained—and the BOSS GETS CHEAP MEN in the FACTORY.

Low rents and cheap living means that wages will go down; the price of wage slaves is lowered and the BOSS GETS THE BENEFIT.

There is only one thing that is starving, sweating and killing you and

International Socialist Review 11 (July 1910): 11–12.

me. That thing is wage-slavery. Do not waste any time boosting reformers. Do not waste any energy making a fat job for the other fellow. Nothing can help you and me permanently as long as a few men own the factories, the mills and the mines.

We MAKE ALL the great and beautiful things in the world and the boss says these things are His. He pays us only enough to feed ourselves, to get us a few cheap hand-me-downs and a shelter in some cheap lodging house.

But supposing we continued to MAKE all the useful and beautiful things we make now and KEPT THEM ourselves or received equal value for them! The only reason you and I work for the boss is because the BOSS owns the MILL. Suppose WE OWNED THE MILL—you and I and thousands of our fellow workers. Suppose we COLLECTIVELY owned the factories and the mines. You know we would never dig up all the things we made and the value we created to hand over to somebody who didn't work.

Socialism means the collective ownership BY the WORKERS of the MINES, the MILLS, the FACTORIES and the LAND, to be used FOR the benefit of the WORKERS.

Think this over. Socialism means the value of the things made in the factory FOR the MEN who work in the factory. It means nothing left for the old boss unless he takes a job beside you and PRODUCES something.

Join the socialist party—the international organization of the working class for the abolition of capitalism. There are ten of us workers to one boss. If we unite, we can own the whole world. Division alone can defeat us.

Think it over. Study up on the subject. You CAN'T lose by becoming a socialist unless you are a capitalist—and the socialists propose to give the capitalists JOBS—so even HE will GAIN SOMETHING.

Unite with your fellow-workers into one great organization of the workers. Alone we can accomplish nothing; united the world is ours!

Are You a Socialist?

IF YOU working men and women understood what socialism really is and means you would flock into the Socialist movement like a policeman going out to get his share in a graft divide. You would scheme just as hard for the advancement of the Socialist movement as any capitalist

International Socialist Review 12 (August 1911): 106–7.

ever schemed and sweat and fought for profits. You would cling to Socialism like a starving dog hangs to a bone, BECAUSE SOCIALISM IS THE ONLY HOPE IN THE WORLD FOR THE WORKING CLASS.

But you are an intelligent workingman. You have been fooled too long to be satisfied with WORDS. You want proofs. You want to know now what Socialism proposes to do. You want to be SHOWN.

Socialism is the international movement of the working class to abolish the wage system. It is a revolutionary movement OF THE WORKERS, BY the workers and FOR the workers. And these workers are not to be side-tracked by anything under the heavens.

They propose that every working man and every working woman shall get the full value of the things they make. They do not intend to leave any rake-off or profits or velvet for those who do not work.

You know that you work for a boss because he owns the factory or the mine or the mill in which you work. If he were a penniless workingman and your father had died leaving you the owner of the mill or the factory HE WOULD HAVE COME TO YOU FOR A JOB. You would be his master. he would have to work for you or for some other boss in order to get wages to LIVE.

The man who works for wages is a slave. He is worse than a slave, for a slave çan always look to his master to feed, clothe and house him. The wage-worker is forced to get a job—to sell his working strength to a boss or beg, starve or steal.

Men and women can never be free or independent as long as they have to beg the idlers for a chance to work. The man who owns your job owns you. Generally he will pay you barely enough to live on, while he keeps for himself all the things you make.

And we workers make everything in the world. There is nothing fine, valuable, beautiful, or useful that is used by men and women, no matter who they are, that is not made by the hands and the brains of work-ingmen or women.

But we are not permitted to enjoy these things. The bosses claim them all. They only give to us (in wages) enough to eke out a poor existence.

The whole secret of our slavery lies in the fact that a few people OWN THE FACTORIES, the MINES, the MILLS, the LANDS and the RAILROADS.

Socialism proposes that the workers who operate the industries shall OWN them collectively—that men and women shall *work for themselves* and shall own the things they make without DIVIDING UP with any idle prop-erty owners. Socialism proposes that the workers themselves shall be the collective owners of the factories, mines, mills, lands and railroads.

When you are joint owner of a mine, you will always have a job in that mine. And the coal or gold you dig will be your own property and not the property of any BOSS.

This is Socialism in a nutshell. If you are a miserable workman living from hand to mouth and in constant fear of losing your job, it ought to sound good to you.

Socialism will give every worker a job and every idler a chance to do some useful, honest work, if he wants to share in the good things workingmen and women produce.

Study Socialism. Send for our book catalogue. Read up on this subject. Socialism is the movement of *your* class, the WORKING CLASS. Join it and help yourself and every other workingman and woman to free themselves from wage-slavery.

Why the Socialist Party Is Different

Why is the Socialist party different from the Republican and Democratic parties? And why should workingmen and women join the Socialist party and its candidates? These are questions that intelligent workers are asking everywhere and that Socialists will have to answer more often than usual during the coming presidential campaign.

We are going to give you a few plain facts and we want you to think them over and talk them over. We want you to find out the aims of Socialism and decide whether the Socialist party will be of benefit to you or whether the old parties will serve you best.

Read the Socialist Party Platform. Compare it with the platform of the Republican and Democratic parties. Read our magazines and buy a few Socialist pamphlets and find out what Socialism means and stands for.

We all know how fertile the old parties have been with PROMISES to the working class, in the past, and how effective in making laws for the benefit of the employing or capitalist class. They have failed you upon every possible occasion. We want you to consider the Socialist program for a while.

1. The aims of Socialism are always in the interest of the working class.

2. Workingmen and women contribute to and conduct our year-long campaign of education. The campaign funds of the Republican and Democratic parties are contributed by such men as E. H. Harriman, J. P. Morgan, John D. Rockefeller, Jim Hill, the Swifts and the Armours.

3. You will find that the Socialists are working men and women fight-

---

International Socialist Review 13 (August 1912): 157.

ing the battles of the WORKING class, while the Republican and Democratic parties are serving the MEN WHO EMPLOY AND ROB YOU.

The factory owners, the mill bosses, the mine operators, have had old party officials serving them long enough. If you workingmen unite in the Socialist party you can elect men from your own ranks to SERVE YOUR INTERESTS.

The working class has nothing in common with other classes in society. We know that any newspaper, any magazine, or any movement that is financed by the employing class is going to serve those who grow rich on our labor.

Sometimes you may see Socialists in office who are trying to lighten the burdens of the workers by reform legislation, such as shortening the hours of labor—giving you an eight hour, instead of a ten or twelve hour day.

But these reform measures are not the essentials of Socialism. The Republican party might make legal the Eight Hour Day. The Democratic party, or a reform party, might pass laws to prevent very young children working in factories. It may be that when the old parties see the workers joining a party of their own, they will give us a few sops to keep us from the REAL BUSINESS OF SOCIALISM.

The real business of Socialism is to abolish a society that is based on the wages system. It proposes that the working class shall take over all the great industries, the mines, mills, the factories, the land and the railroads; it means that these industries shall be owned and managed by the workers who use them and that every working man and woman shall receive the full value of his product, without handing over any profits to any boss.

The man who owns a cotton factory today employs men and women and children to work FOR HIM. He pays them starvation wages while he makes millions of dollars profits on the cloth THEY WEAVE.

It is ownership of the factory that makes one man a rich and idle employer and the man, who has no property, a wage slave.

Socialism stands for the ownership of the factory by the factory workers. It means the overthrow of the wage system. This is the real essence of Socialism.

Why Catholic Workers Should Be Socialists

Our Catholic fellow workers ought to become Socialists for the same reason that all workers belong in the Socialist movement. It does not matter whether you are a Catholic, or a Methodist, a Baptist or a Presbyterian, an Italian, Irishman or an American, a Japanese or a Negro—if you are a working man or a working woman your place is in the Socialist movement.

The place of every working man and woman is in the Socialist movement because Socialism is the one movement in the world devoted to *protecting* the interests of the working class, to aiding the workers in securing shorter hours, higher wages and first, last and all the time to helping them in their efforts to improve their material living conditions.

Helping the workers is the every day aim of Socialism, but the great goal towards which Socialists are working is a new society in which *every worker shall receive the value of his product.* . . .

In other words, we are working for a society where the man who plants a crop shall reap his own harvest, where the man who builds houses shall receive those houses, or the value of those houses; where every worker shall receive the value of the things he makes.

Today the workers sow all the wheat, make the bread, build the homes for the world, dig the coal, run the railroads to *make profits for the boss.* We intend to stop making profits and working *for him* and begin to *make things for ourselves.* We shall work *for ourselves,* our wives and our families instead of working for *a boss.* We will give the boss a chance to *work for* himself. . . .

We do not intend to permit anybody to make any *profit out of you or me.* We shall organize with the other workers of the world, Atheist, Presbyterian, Italian, German, Catholic, Chinaman, Negro—all together into one great working class union. We shall ask every working man and woman in the world to join us. We shall guarantee easy work, short hours, a comfortable living and old age incomes to every useful member of society.

Socialism means that *you* shall receive the value of your work and *not* an idle boss who performs no useful toil. It means that you will receive twice as much for your labor as I will if *you work twice as long.*

THE CHURCH AND SOCIALISM

You will often hear priests and clergymen speaking on Socialism. Sometimes they do not understand it and sometimes they misrepresent it.

We are going to *abolish poverty from the face of* the earth. What have they

---

Why Catholic Workers Should Be Socialists (Chicago: Charles H. Kerr & Co., 1914), 1–4, 9–16, 18–25.

to say about that? Are they with us? We need soldiers in the great army of the revolution. Will the churches join us in the great crusade?

Nobody can help you and me and our bosses at the same time. Because every time we secure shorter hours or higher wages it means lower dividends for the boss, and whenever the boss can cut our wages or force us to work longer hours, it means more profits for him.

The church must help those who work against those *who sponge off* the workers. The church must lend its aid to those who toil, in their struggles with the idlers who *do no useful work.*

BREAKING UP THE HOME

Every day we see homes being broken up all around us. The *homes* of *thousands of workers are broken up every day.* Fathers are forced to leave their families and go to distant states *to get a job;* mothers are compelled to leave their babes and earn money in factories or mills to support them. Little children, who ought to be in school, have to go to work to keep the *wolf from the door.*

Low wages, uncertain jobs and the *profit system* are breaking up the homes of working people faster and faster every day.

Poverty breaks up a million homes every year.

The security of your home depends upon your job and that is uncertain, because your *boss controls your job.* You are his working slave and he throws you out of work to *starve whenever he so desires.*

Socialists are organizing the working class to own their own mills, factories, mines, farms, and shops so that every worker will be certain of a job as long as he wants it. . . .

MORE ABOUT SOCIALISM AND THE FAMILY

Judging from what some of our uninformed Catholic friends claim, one would imagine that all the millions of prostitutes in the world today were members of the Socialist Party. Unfortunately we have never known a Public Woman who was a member of our organization.

If prostitutes realized that Socialism is the only movement that will make prostitution unnecessary, they would flock to the movement like starving men to a feast, in order to help abolish the living Hell that the *present* system of society has thrust them into.

Over and over again, we meet people who say, "Does Socialism mean 'Free Love'?"

We wonder again if the implication is that we wish to impose a universal system of prostitution or Mormonism upon society!

Understand, once and for all, we are opposed to a system of Society that, in the phrase of the streets, stands for "Bought Love" or purchased sexual intercourse. Socialists insist that the present system of society which makes unemployment the portion of hundreds of thousands of workers *all the time,* and of millions some of the time, that makes the means of life for the great majority of the people dependent upon the will of a few multimillionaires—such a system is the soil from which prostitution has actually sprung. . . .

The Socialist Party will pass no laws to drive prostitution from the city streets. It will give the Public Woman a home of her own to go to. It will give steady work, easy, useful work at high pay, short hours, leisure and independence to all men and all women, and prostitution, or *"bought love,"* will become a dread evil of the past.

Free women and free men do not sell themselves either mentally or physically.

The Churches are not responsible for the prostitution of the world today except in so far as they oppose the only movement that will abolish prostitution. What is the command of the Church to the prostitute today? Perhaps it tells these women to "go to work." But lack of work is the fundamental cause of prostitution.

If you stand for the present system which means unemployment, uncertain jobs, hunger in the midst of the plenty that you have produced, increasing wealth of the idlers and increasing poverty of the toilers, then you stand for prostitution and the conditions that are the cause of thievery and crime. Then you stand for homes "broken up" before they are ever made.

WHAT WE STAND FOR

No Socialist Party of any country ever held any program for governing or regulating or changing or continuing the Institution of the Family. As Karl Marx and Frederick Engels have well said, the future society for which we are striving—the future of government—if you so wish to call it—will be a Bureau for the Administration of *Industry.*

In other words, the brain workers and hand workers will collectively own and control the factories, mines, the land, mills and shops. The function of government will then be the scientific production and distribution of ample, wholesome food for all, the making of beautiful and abundant clothing, the building of homes for each and every human being.

The Industrial Bureau, or Socialist government, has no laws to enforce regarding family life. Its duty will be to see that there are ample goods produced to feed, clothe, house and insure the comfort and independence of every man and woman.

Do not be deceived by what the most exalted personage has to say about Socialism. He may be in error. Read the Party Platform and think for yourself and when any misinformed speaker tells you what he thinks we stand for, read our program—our Platform.

No Socialist organization ever had a program in regard to the regulation of the Family Institution. That is not the function of Socialism. It is our purpose to systematize society in such a way that every man and woman who works shall enjoy all of the good things of life.

Every socialist believes that the relations of men and women, of husband and wife, are the concern of themselves alone. The Socialist Party has nothing to say on the subject of Marriage. This, too, is a private matter over which we desire no jurisdiction.

Once more, Socialism has no concern in the private affairs of any individual, be he Socialist, Catholic, Jew or Mohammedan, or any member of any other organization. Our affair is taking over the administration of the industries and seeing to it that no portion of the product of any workers shall be appropriated by any capitalist through the private ownership of those things on which our lives depend. . . .

DON'T AGREE

A Catholic lecturer recently declared that if you would put ten socialists in a room, no two of them would agree. This is true. No two persons on earth agree upon every subject. I have never met ten Catholics or ten Jews or ten Negroes who could agree upon every subject.

It is not necessary that the members of an organization should agree upon all subjects. It is only necessary that they agree upon those things that they are united to accomplish, on the ends they are striving to attain.

. . . The Catholic and the Baptist prostitutes doubtless find grave points of difference from the other members of their respective churches. No two Catholics agree on all subjects.

And Socialists are just like other folks. In our Party organization every member has an equal voice and vote with every other member and one and all are united on the essentials of Socialism—in the aims and ends of the socialist movement.

We are one and all united in our purpose to overthrow the wages system. We are united to promote a society that shall give to the workers the full value of their products.

Here and there we advocate reforms that we believe will educate and benefit the workers. Many of us differ in our views as to the merits of these measures. If they will teach the workers to think for themselves, we are for them. If they mean a higher standard of living for the working class, we put our strength behind them. If they show the workers how they may further advance their own interests, we put our shoulders to the wheel.

Sometimes we disagree over the best means to advance our ultimate purpose. But *about the end there is no dispute.*

Socialism is the greatest movement for materially improving the living conditions of the human race the world has ever known. It is international in scope. It has millions of never-sleeping educators and propagandists in every country on the globe.

It is true that on one hundred subjects we fail to agree. My German comrade inclines to the belief that the Fatherland produces the greatest scientists, while my French sister declares that from France come the master scientists. Our Catholic and religious co-workers enter into innumerable wordy engagements with our materialist friends in the Party. Among the Finns, Hungarians and Bohemians there is much friendly rivalry over the accomplishment of tasks all but impossible to any save a socialist.

In the Socialist Party the vivisectionist disputes with the anti-vivisectionists; trade unionist and industrial unionist discuss, with fine spirit, the merits of their respective unions at the same time. The Marxian and the Bernsteinian find forty points of difference. Upon the hundred points we debate and differentiate—but upon the *aims of Socialism*— there we clasp hands with brother and sister of every land, of every color, of every creed—united in one unalterable purpose: the *overthrow* of the *wages system* and the *full value* of their *products* for the *working class.*

Like other folks, we socialists differ on every subject under the sun. We even differ sometimes on the best way to obtain Socialism, but we are always united on the great goal—The abolition of Poverty from the face of the earth!

WAR AND PATRIOTISM

. . . [S]ocialists are unpatriotic because we have no country. We shall boast of our own Fatherland when we have made America the real land of those who do the work—in America.

We do not believe in war. No socialist would shoot down his German shopmate who works beside him in the mill. Why then should he murder his German brother in war?

The German comrade across the water is probably just as brave and kindly a friend as the German he has gone out on strike with. We have found our French Catholic neighbor a generous and pleasant comrade. We do not believe his brother in France is any the less worthy because he has not crossed the Atlantic and taken out his nationalization papers. We would just as soon kill one as the other. In either case the world would probably be the poorer by one honest worker whose interests are identical with our own.

The working class has no country. Every country has been grabbed up by the bosses—field, city and even cemetery—long before we appeared on the boards.

A rented flat, a rented patch of land—these are a portion of the owners' country—not yours nor mine. When a man is out of work he is driven from city to city. He has no place to lay his head. The constant order hurled upon him by the officials of town and country, usually with brutal blows to accompany the command, is, "Move on." These men have no "country."

It is natural that the property owner should be patriotic. He owns property and desires to protect it. But it is foolish to expect intelligent workingmen to fight to protect the property of which *the boss has robbed him.* Socialism is broader than any nation just as the Catholic Church is broader than any nation. We have no foe save all those who live without toiling, save those who rob and exploit the workers. They are the Foreigners. Every workingman and woman in the world is our Countryman and Countrywoman.

It does not so much concern us that a King sits upon the throne in England—the English worker eats or starves at the withdrawal of a chance to work by the English boss. If this English worker crosses the border into France or Germany, he will still find that he must find a boss to whom he can sell his strength, or his brains, if he is to earn money for food and lodging. The same is true in America, in Australia, in New Zealand. Ever the workingman is commanded to "Move on" when he can find no work. Where is this man's country?. . .

We might quote from hundreds of articles by eminent Catholics which prove that the Catholic Church is an *international* organization and absolutely lacking in patriotism. But we have no quarrel with the Catholic Church on this score. The socialist position is precisely the same. Our movement is an international one. It is an international, working class movement for the *material* advancement and emancipation of the workers of the world. . . .

PRIVATE PROPERTY

. . . Socialism will abolish the private ownership of the necessities of life by all individuals. It will make it impossible for any landlord to own *your* home or my home. Under Socialism no man or woman will be permitted to grab up a hundred houses so that they can force us to pay rent in order to live.

Socialism will abolish the private ownership of the great factories, the shops, the woolen mills and flour mills, the privately owned railroads and private ownership in land.

The things which we use collectively shall be owned collectively by those who perform any useful work.

And all the things *which we use privately,* we shall own privately. No man will be permitted to own privately anything that the lives of men depend upon. Then every man and woman will have an opportunity to produce and enjoy all the good things of life.

There will be larger herds of cattle on the plains, better and more beautiful clothes, more comfortable homes for every one, more luxuries *for all those who perform some useful function in society.*

There will be Old Age Incomes and Incomes for the Sick and the opportunity for the broadest education for all the youth in the land. The glad day will come when no landlord shall own the house in which you dwell, when no boss shall be able to deny any man or woman the right to work in the factory, mine and mill, to produce the necessities and luxuries of life.

CONFISCATION

Today everywhere in the world where men and women and little children are working for wages, you will see the master class and the working class fighting for the *products of the laborers.*

The bosses are trying to keep more of the coal we have dug, more of the clothes we have made, more of the foods we have produced. And we are fighting to get more of the value of our products.

The workers have produced every piece of cloth in the world today. It is their hands that have gone into the bowels of the earth to bring up the coal that warms the people of the world; it is our hands that have built the houses and that have built the factories, shops, mills and railroads. It is the hand of Labor that feeds, clothes and houses the world.

We need collective ownership of the factories and of the land and mines, of the shops and mills and railroads so that every man and woman shall have opportunity to work and enjoy the fruits of his labor.

Today we see the employers of labor confiscating *our* products for their own profit. The entire wealth which they possess has *been confiscated from the working class. . . .*

SOCIALISM AND LABOR

The Socialist Party is an organization of the working class for the overthrow of the wages system. This is its goal. In the meantime you will find us everywhere and at all times aiding the workers in every struggle they wage against the master class to improve their conditions, to shorten hours, to broaden education, to abolish child labor or increase wages. . . .

Whenever and wherever there is an election or a strike, you will find the Socialist Party throwing open its press to help the workers beat the bosses.

In an election you will find the socialist candidate advocating laws for shorter hours, better safety conditions, sanitation for the workers, abolition of child labor—conditions that will make for higher wages—working for any measure that will benefit the working class.

In all our struggles when has the Catholic Church or any other Church *ever* opened the columns of its newspapers to help us get more *pay from the bosses?* When has the Church stood faithfully for those who work? Has the Catholic Church ever dispatched a car load of provisions to a group of hungry strikers? Has it ever donated as much as ten dollars to help the workers win *any* strike or any election? Has it backed the socialist candidates in an election because it knew they would serve the interests of the *workers?*

No organization can help your boss and you at the same time. When your boss cuts your wages, that means more money for him. When you force a wage increase, there remains less for the boss. Longer hours of labor mean higher profits for the boss; a shorter working day will lower his dividends. Nobody can help you and me and our bosses at the same time.

The Church will have to help us or it will help those who rob us. If the Churches are our real friends, they will help us to throw off the bondage of a boss. They will serve us in all our elections, in every time of trouble—with their newspapers, their influence and with cash donations. . . .

OUR ATTITUDE TOWARD THE CHURCHES

As stated in preceding pages, the Socialist Party *officially* regards religion as a private matter. The official attitude toward the Churches is the same.

The Churches themselves, however, have never remained neutral in any historic labor struggle. Only a few hundred years ago slavery was sanctioned and upheld by the Catholic Church as an institution ordained of God. The slave who rebelled against his master was severely punished by the mother Church.

The Catholic Church advocated and maintained the serfdom of our fathers as a divine institution.

Personally, we believe the Churches will neither desire nor find it possible to remain neutral in the great struggles being waged for emancipation by the working class today.

The Catholic Church is already advising its members to support certain candidates and certain reactionary measures at the elections. This Church which, only a few months ago, was severely denouncing woman suffrage, is now urging all its women communicants who have been granted the franchise to go to the polls and vote.

You know the Socialist Party is ready to serve the working class at every election and at all other times. But if you doubt, read our platforms, our principles, our programs and see where we stand on every subject. Do not take the word of *any* individuals. *Use your own mind.* See where we stand on every issue. *Watch and find out.*

And then see what is the attitude of your Church. Is it upholding the socialist candidates who represent the interests of labor or is it telling you to vote for the man who *serves the interests* of your *bosses?*

Will it support the candidates who mean to maintain the present system of society with its poverty, unemployment, boss-owned jobs, crime, misery and prostitution?

What is said in these pages about the Socialist Party and the Catholic Church and any other Churches does not much matter. *But it does matter that you watch the Churches and the Socialist Party and all other parties and find out which is really helping the working class!*

Think this over; read up on Socialism and watch closely at every election, at every strike, at the boycotts and lock-outs. The most important thing in the world is that you should think these things out for yourself.

Will the Churches change their general attitude in the strikes that are constantly occurring between the Owning Class and the Producing Class, and lend their press, their influence, donating funds and food to the strikers?

To my mind, the attitude of the Socialist Party toward *religion* will remain what it is today. But I believe that our attitude toward the *Churches* will be determined by the attitude of the Churches toward the working class.

If they fight *against* the working class, we shall continue to fight *with* the workers in all their struggles for improvement.

If they betray our class, we, at least, shall prove faithful to it. If any Church interprets the teachings of Jesus as a command to help the downtrodden and despoiled to emancipation and shall take up the cudgels in our behalf, we shall not forget.

But we, the workers, shall be free!

Through the long and weary centuries we have fed the world, clothed and housed it. And we have been starved, murdered and betrayed. We have waged continual war for freedom from those who have enslaved us.

Long ago our grandfathers threw off the yoke of the masters who held them in chattel slavery. Again in the eighteenth century our fathers vanquished the feudal lords and were no longer serfs—tied to the seigneurs' lands.

Time and again have we been sold out by our pretended friends, misled by ambitious leaders, been betrayed by those who have sworn to befriend us.

And yet the light of hope has never failed us. We have found our comrades true; we have learned to trust in our own strength! And the day will soon come when we shall emerge victorious in our last great battle with those who exploit and rob us.

We workers shall be free from the boss-controlled job, from poverty, hunger, unemployment—from the criminal system of wage slavery that today endures.

And if any church ally itself with the forces of robbery and oppression, it it dares to stand for all these evils, if it dares to block the path of Progress and Freedom for those who toil—we shall fight the more wisely, having learned the forces that oppose us; we shall fight the more bravely until all our enemies go down into shameful defeat and the Working Class shall come into its own!

5

Open the Factories

THE last—and among the most forcefully argued—of Marcy's many pamphlets concerned with improving the lot of working men and women was *Open the Factories,* excerpts from which appear below. Contending that political democracy is nothing more than a mockery, as long as the nation's workers "are bowed beneath the yoke of industrial autocracy," Marcy demands in this brief pamphlet that the government "open the factories" and make certain that work is given to every man and woman in the United States who wants it.

In 1921, when the pamphlet was written, the Socialist party's prospects were far different than they had been in 1912. Persecution resulting from its opposition to World War I hurt the party: Debs and many others were imprisoned, Socialist literature was barred from the mails, and vigilante actions had weakened its outlying bodies, especially in the western states. But it was the Bolshevik Revolution in Russia and not the war that led to the party's loss of authenticity as a movement of radical action. The problem was not the revolution itself—this was hailed by every faction of the party, including "evolutionists" who had denounced the doctrine of violence—but the question whether it provided a model for the United States. The left wing, which had long disapproved of social reform within capitalism and opposed parliamentary socialist action, believed that the revolution was a model and it succumbed to the illusion that revolution in this country was imminent. The leaders of the party took a contrasting position. They neither accepted the view that America was ripe for revolution nor gave in to demands that the party be restructured along Leninist lines. The result was a split in the Socialist movement. By the late summer of 1919 there were three parties where there had been one—the Socialist Party of America, the Communist Party, and the Communist Labor Party—and none of them were very strong. Within a year after the split they had only thirty-six thousand members among them; by 1921 the Socialist party had dwindled to less than fourteen thousand members. Depite some revival during the early

1930s, it never regained either its popular base or the electoral appeal it had enjoyed earlier.

The IWW at the time Marcy wrote *Open the Factories* was also a mere shell of what it had been before the war. Although, unlike the Socialist party, the union had hedged on the war issue, federal and state governments feared it nonetheless as a threat to national security. As a consequence, over two hundred IWW officials were arrested, indicted, and convicted under the Espionage and Sedition Acts. After 1919, continuing government pressure, along with successful competition from communists, further crippled the union. By the mid-1920s the heart had gone out of it; the IWW was never the same again.

Open the Factories

TWO KINDS OF AUTOCRACY

There are two kinds of autocracy in the world today. The German kaiser was a political autocrat, but one of the first and foremost aims of his whole life was to do all he could to see that the German people had food, clothing, homes to sleep in, and work to enable them to pay for all these things.

We rejoice that the days of the kaiser's political autocracy are dead and gone, but we also think it is about time that we all gave some thought to the industrial autocrats that rule the lives of the working class in our own country. Do you know who these autocrats are?

They are the owners of the shops, the factories, the mills and mines who say when men shall have work, when the factories and plants shall close down and when, if workingmen cannot get other jobs, under other industrial autocrats, they are compelled to beg, to rob or to starve!

Industrial autocracy is quite as bad as political autocracy, if not worse. . . .

Nothing on earth stands in the way of comfort and happiness, jobs and *plenty for every willing man and woman* in America except the insatiable *greed of the industrial autocrats* and the criminal negligence of the politicians and the people themselves.

If your neighbor came to you and said: "My wife and my children are starving," you would send them food and be happy to be able to help them.

But what about the factory owners, the mill and mine owners who have piled up billions of dollars in profits during the war and now close their plants, throwing men out of work to starve?

If, as we have been taught to believe, the United States Government is actually a democratic government, why should it not act in this tragic emergency and consider the lives and the welfare of the many instead of the *property* and the *profits* of the few? Under Government supervision millions of dollars are being collected to feed the hungry in China and in Austria, *what is the matter that the Government officials do not act to help out hungry people at home?*

Why should not the Government *open the factories,* the *mills* and the *mines* and permit the jobless to go into them and produce the things they are suffering for?

Open the Factories (Chicago: Charles H. Kerr & Co., 1921), 3–7, 12–13, 22–23, 31.

Or *is* a political democracy merely a *farce* so long as men are bowed beneath the yoke of *industrial autocracy?*

Is America the sort of a country that will permit a few millionaires to say when workmen shall have work and when they shall starve?

OUR DEMANDS ARE:

Open the factories, the *mills* and the *mines* and *check this deadly crisis of unemployment* and *hunger!*

Give work (or *food, clothing* and *shelter*) to *every man and woman in the United States who wants them!* . . .

ONE THING SACRED.

Do you know that there is only one thing sacred in the whole "democratic" world today? And can you guess what that thing is? Perhaps you will imagine, as I used to believe, that human life is sacred. But if you will consider the subject for a few minutes you will see that such a guess is all wrong.

Human life and human welfare *ought* to be sacred. It ought to be that every man and woman would sacrifice luxuries and unnecessary things, and even their own comfort to save human life. But when you have thought about the matter a little while you will realize that the *lives* of the working class are held cheaper than anything a manufacturer has to see on his factory shelves. Private property is the one thing which we are taught at all times to regard as utterly sacred.

A man may kill a starving workman who is unable to get a job and who steals something to eat. Which is one indication of the relative value of human life and human property.

Second: There are at least ninety-nine laws written on the statute books for the protection of private property to every one written to protect human lives, which is quite damning proof that the august lawmakers of America regard a sack of flour, or a sugar-cured ham, or a pair of trousers as being about ninety times as valuable as a human life.

The police department is nearly always used, and primarily used, to protect property and to protect the boss's right to acquire more private property.

Ask the first policeman you meet to help you secure some food. Tell him you are out of work and ill and starving. Assure him this is a case of life or death to you. I think nearly all of them will ask you if you think they are a charity bureau and threaten to run you in if you don't beat it and quit blocking the traffic.

But let a millionaire secure a majority of the stock of copper mines or oil wells in Mexico by bribing some corrupt politician, and let the Mexican people seek to get back their own again, and the millionaire property owner will appeal to Congress and the President for a million soldiers to go down into Mexico to fight and to die, if need be, to make his *loot secure to him.*

Did you ever hear of a Congressman or a "statesman" proposing any laws whereby hungry and starving people shall be fed? They are elected to protect the property of the owners and are too busy passing laws that will prohibit workers from striking for higher wages, to have any time for such unimportant details as *human starvation.*

That is the way it is with the politicians and the newspaper editors. If you tell them about hungry school children or penniless men and women begging for a chance to work, they are too busy to hear because human life is held too cheap. But everybody has a heart somewhere— even the newspaper editors and the politicians. Let anybody touch a rich man's pocket book (by hurting his profits or destroying his property) and they are willing to send you and me to fight and to die to protect these *things.* It is not *life* they care for, but *things.* . . .

WHAT IS CAPITAL?

You never knew a worker who got rich by saving his wages. Men *began* to grow rich by getting hold of the natural resources of a land. They obtained control of these resources by accident, by bribery, by purchase before anybody knew their true value and often by gift from some corrupt politicians. They held on to these natural resources whether they were land, water rights, timberlands, mines, railroad lands or oil wells, and they proceeded to *hold up everybody* who had to have those things.

They grew rich through these hold-ups and had more capital to invest.

And what does a capitalist do when he has money to invest? He puts it in mills, factories, shops, etc., etc. Then he hires workers to run the factories and pays them wages which equal less than one-fifth of the value of the things they make in them. And at the end of the year the capitalist finds that the workers have made 20 to 50 per cent on his investment for him. Occasionally they even double his investment or treble his investment for him in *one year.*

In other words, the men and woman who work in the factories or shops soon double the capital of the employer who secures these profits (or capital) by paying his workers about one-fifth of the value of the things they produce. You can call it a skin game, a double cross or sheer robbery. There is no question about its being a case of you workers getting one dollar for every five dollars' worth of goods you make.

Well, then, the next year this capitalist has more money to put into some new enterprise and he puts the money you have been simple enough to let him make off you in new factories or new mills. He puts his loot into new enterprises and hires more workers for wages, to run the new factories and produce more commodities and *more profits* (or more *capital*) *for him.*

And again he pays his workers one dollar for every five dollars' worth of goods they make, so that, in a year or two or three, he finds that they have *again doubled his capital* and that he has more money to invest in new factories the next year. And so on.

In other words, *the capital of the millionaires comes out of your sweat and your labor.* You produce much for little. You are stung and the big thieves get away with the swag, with a thousand laws to protect them in their lootings.

Do you see how *capital* is the product of the workers and should *belong* to the working class? . . .

WHAT DO YOU THINK ABOUT IT?

Whoever you are, what do you think should be done in the present crisis in our own country? After long years of toil and service, shall useful men and women and their families be permitted to starve through lack of work? Or shall the factories, shops, the mines and mills be opened to permit these hungry folks to produce the things they need?

Which is more sacred—private profits or *human life?*

6
Socialist Stories for Young and Old

MARY Marcy's skill as a writer is revealed not only in her factual treatises on economic and political questions, but also in her many fictional works. The short stories reprinted here as the next three selections satirize the capitalist system, emphasizing in particular the evils of bourgeois "charity" as opposed to proletarian unity.

Although Charles H. Kerr & Company was not the major publisher of Socialist novels during the first two decades of the century (that distinction, interestingly enough, belonged to the Macmillan Company, a firm that was not radical at all), it did publish a small number of them, including Marcy's *Out of the Dump*. Excerpts from the latter, which first appeared serially in the *International Socialist Review,* constitute the fourth selection. Written in the first person, the novel relates the experiences of a family living in a certain wretched portion of the stockyards region of Chicago known locally as "The Dump." It thinly veils references to the Armour Company, and tells of the death of the father of the family as the result of the packing company's lack of safety precautions; of the efforts of the mother to keep the family together; of their distressing experience with organized charity, and of their ups and downs through illness, death and varied fortunes. At the novel's end, the eldest son, similar to Jurgis Rudkus, the principal character in Upton Sinclair's *The Jungle,* is converted to Socialism.

When *Out of the Dump* was issued as a separate publication the year following its serialization in the *Review,* it included illustrations by Marcy's friend Ralph Chaplin (1887–1961), whose participation in Socialist circles had led to his appointment at age twenty-one to Kerr & Company's board of directors. During the next half-dozen years, he traveled widely, living for brief periods in Mexico, West Virginia, Ohio, and Canada. In 1913, while in Cleveland, Ohio, he joined the IWW. Returning to Chicago in 1915, he wrote the words to the famous song "Solidarity Forever" and soon became a close associate of IWW leader William D. "Big Bill" Haywood, who appointed him editor of the union's paper, *Solidarity,* in 1917.

As a result of his activities opposing World War I, Chaplin was one of 166 IWW members arrested by the federal government in September 1917. The next year, following a five-month trial, he was convicted of conspiracy to violate the wartime Espionage and Sedition Acts and sentenced to twenty years in the federal prison at Leavenworth, Kansas. In 1919, while out on bail pending an appeal, he joined the newly created Communist party. His appeal was rejected by the Supreme Court and he entered Leavenworth in April 1921, remaining there until 1923 when President Harding commuted his sentence to time already served. It was at Leavenworth that he received the news of Marcy's death.

After his release from prison, Chaplin became increasingly disillusioned with his radical past. Although he returned to work for the IWW, he sought to steer it in a technocratic direction, to transform the organization into something of a research bureau, which would collect and publish information on the American economy. Never enthusiastic about the Russian Bolsheviks, he broke completely with communism in 1928, the year of Haywood's death in the Soviet Union. During the thirties, he served as the editor for several labor magazines, and in 1937 he moved to the west coast to work for groups in the labor movement opposed to Harry Bridges, the left-wing leader of the International Longshoremen's and Warehousemen's Union. A strong supporter of the American role in World War II, Chaplin became in later years a chronicler of the IWW past.

The final selection from Marcy's fictional prose is comprised of four of her "Stories of the Cave People" (eleven in all), tales of prehistoric man written for children. An attempt to embody the anthropological viewpoint of the noted American ethnologist Lewis H. Morgan (1818–81), the stories were published in book form after appearing separately in the *International Socialist Review* beginning in 1909. Not surprisingly, given their content, the stories received a mixed reaction from reviewers. For example, the *Boston Transcript,* reflecting conservative opinion, recognized their "considerable ingenuity," but challenged sharply their secular premise, while the *Industrial Pioneer,* a monthly issued by the IWW, voiced the opinion that, as "a substitute for the insipid fairy tales of the Sunday school type," they "cannot be recommended too highly."

The stories "The Ornament of Big Nose" and "Little Laughing Boy" are of particular interest for their depiction of man's physical evolution from ape-like tree dwellers to cave dwellers who had "learned to walk erect, on two legs" and whose "arms . . . had grown shorter as they ceased to swing themselves constantly, from tree to tree." The concluding story, describing how One Ear became the cave people's first priest, endorses unequivocally Marx's proposition that "man makes religion, religion does not make man." Like Marx, Marcy was convinced that religion arose from the helplessness of primitive man when confronted with the elemental forces of nature. Not understanding nature—but, rather, regarding it as an overpowering, mystifying presence—primitive man worshiped it, thus giving birth to religion. Hence, religion originated as the fantastic reflection in men's minds of the external forces that controlled their daily life. Or, as Marx's friend and collaborator Friedrich Engels put it (rather more bluntly) in *Feuerbach, the Roots of Socialist Philosophy*, religion had "its roots in the limited and ignorant ideas of savagery," "in certain erroneous and barbaric conceptions."[1] Later, as man came to understand nature and brought natural forces under his control, religion continued as a means of placating equally mysterious and hostile social forces.

Note

1. Friedrich Engels, *Feuerbach, the Roots of Socialist Philosophy*, trans. Austin Lewis (Chicago: Charles H. Kerr & Co., 1903), 57, 118.

William the Faithful

Mrs. Pitzer was a widow with seven children, who lived in Lucasville, Ohio. She had Heart Trouble, so it was up to her eldest sons, William and Wallace, to hump for the Family Flock.

William was steady and industrious. He kept the books and handled the cash for the Wind Mill Factory at ten dollars a week. Whenever the rent man or the grocer came around, William always was there with the goods.

He spent his evenings steering the little Pitzers through the shoals of Long Division and the intricacies of the Multiplication Table, and whenever he got a half day off he put on his overalls and cut the grass or split kindling for the kitchen stove.

No matter when the call came, he was never asleep at the switch.

Wallace was different. He liked to loaf around the stores and chew tobacco and crack coarse jokes. He stood to win with all the Rough Necks in the county, and Sat Down cheerfully on William like a Wet Sponge.

The neighbors said he was too lazy to take off his clothes when he went to bed and the members of the First Church felt so sorry for Mrs. Pitzer that they thought of Wallace during Protracted Meeting and gave him a special Interest in their Prayers.

One spring Wallace soured on Lucasville, so he pryed open William's bank of mortgage money and went West.

He squatted in Missouri and sent home such Cutting letters that his mother flew into hysterics every time she came across an old piece of Battle Ax.

She said if William had treated Wallace with a little more consideration, he never would have left home.

But Wallace's feet got colder every day. A nice little stream ran through his claim and there were plenty of rocks, but the breezes didn't stir up any gold dust nor did he strike oil. And he found that settlers out West hated a loafer almost as much as they did back in Ohio.

He wrote for money to go home on, but it takes a long time to save $35.50 out of a busy salary of ten dollars a week, and he couldn't find anybody green enough to trade a return ticket for a piece of worthless farm land. So Wallace stuck.

But this is not the end of the story. In a few years a city grew up on the banks of the Kaw and Wallace's land increased in value. He sold part of his claim and put up a store and was known as a "Prominent Citizen." The new year he let go of another square, erected a business block and became a Benefactor.

And when the Street Railway began operations and the Gas Company

---

International Socialist Review 7 (March 1907): 557–58.

was organized, the people elected him mayor and he began to write magazine articles for young men on "How to Succeed."

Last year Wallace was made President of the Commercial Club and the papers still rave over his "Financial Acumen" and his "Wonderful Business Foresight."

Occasionally Lucasville is honored by a visit from its distinguished townsman, when Mrs. Pitzer is moved to chide William for his lack of enterprise. And Wallace hands out advice freely on every side.

All these years William has been doing the Faithful Fido act twelve hours a day at ten dollars a week, for the Wind Mill people. A younger man is Handling the Cash at a bigger salary. But every Christmas the manager comes around and slaps William on the back and says the House needs Faithful Men.

All of which goes to show that Virtue is still its own reward.

How Tom Saved the Business

James Barton, Tom's father, was a business man of the old school. He delivered the kind of goods he sold and he sold the best. Furthermore, he never took an "unfair advantage" of anybody, and his word was "as good as his bond."

For nearly thirty years Mr. Barton had been the "most prominent citizen" in Lucasville. He felt a pardonable pride when the factory was enlarged and the little real estate company and the town banker were forced to put up several rows of new cottages to accommodate the new men who brought their families when they came to work for the factory people. The grocers began to employ new clerks and the village gradually assumed an air of busy industry that delighted Mr. Barton's heart.

The county papers spoke of him as a public benefactor and for many years he was the largest contributor toward the salary of the pastor of the First Congregational Church.

This is the story of his rise. When Tom was a very little shaver and Tom's mother was the neatest and prettiest young wife in the whole state, Jim Barton made the acquaintance of a silent chap who worked near him in the molding rooms. The acquaintance ripened into friendship and when the whistle blew at noon, it came to be the thing for Jim Barton and Sid Mathews to sit outside in the cool and eat their lunch together. Sid's original ideas upon machinery interested Jim, so it came about that when Sid fell upon a bright idea, he wandered over to the cottage to tell Jim Barton about it.

International Socialist Review 9 (February 1909): 598–602.

Secretly Sid planned and schemed and experimented over the biggest thing of all, and when at last his patterns were perfected, the gear ran flawlessly and he rejoiced in the thing he had wrought, Sid sought Jim Barton to tell him the good news.

Although Jim Barton was no mechanical genius, he became so enthusiastic over Sid's invention that he sold off the timber from his land and went to manufacturing at once. They estimated Sid's patent rights to be worth a third of the business, and Sid was to have his share of the profits.

They prospered amazingly. Jim managed the business and Sid puttered around the molding rooms. Occasionally he invented another device—a simpler lever, or a cheaper attachment. These, with his Mathews' Valve patents, he turned over to the company.

Jim Barton was the kindest boss that ever ruled in old Missouri. He loved his men and it was a saying with him "if you make a workingman contented, he'll die for you." The men rarely left his employ.

In '93, during the panic, when the company (of course, it was a stock company by that time) ran very close to the danger line, Jim Barton had a heart-to-heart talk with his men. He hated to do it, he told them, but he would have to cut wages 25 percent or lay off a part of the force. Voluntarily he cut his own salary 25 per cent at the same time. And they tell me, not one of the men would have gone out for even better pay that winter. Nearly every one of them could tell, with a clutch at his heart, of some time of illness or trouble in his little home, when old Jim Barton had knocked at the door and given them a lift over the bad place.

So there was much joy in Jim Barton's life and he went proudly and serenely on his way. Tom went to college, of course, and the first real blow Jim ever had was when Tom decided to go to work for the Harvester Trust. Tom said his father's business methods were out of date.

The next year the orders came more slowly, for the competitors of Barton, Mathews & Co. slashed prices savagely and houses that were willing to pay for the "very best" dwindled about forty per cent.

Mathews had been permanently crippled the year before while experimenting on a new wrinkle in the Mathews Self-Regulator. Nobody knew how he tripped over a wire into the white iron, ready for the molds. Sid's salary went on just the same, but thereafter Jim Barton had to make the fight alone.

Often at night, when his wife lay sleeping, Jim Barton would slip on his bath robe and slippers and steal into the sitting-room and try to figure it out. He worked over the Cost Price. Again and again he figured it over. He could not put out an inferior "grade of make." He simply couldn't. It made the old man groan at the mere thought. "Barton & Mathews' grade has always been the best, and it must keep on," he would say to himself.

Then he would sharpen his pencil and look over the Pay Roll. To be sure there was Sid Mathews still getting his $3,000 a year, but Sid's inventions had MADE the business, and Sid's children had to be sent to school, and—he ran his eyes down over the list. There were Lewis, Morgan, Tucker and three or four others who were old and stiff and not much account, but they all needed jobs DESPERATELY—more than any of the younger men. Besides they had stood by the House in '93. They could not go.

There was the superintendent—in name only, but Mr. Barton wiped his eyes when he thought of the pain faithful Smith would feel if he were laid on the shelf. Thus he ran over the list. The men who were getting too much had families who could not live on less, and no true Christian, Mr. Barton thought, would turn off men because they had grown old.

He always ended by closing the Time Book and running his long, gnarled fingers through his sparse grey hair. Then he would sigh gently and resolve to draw as little money out of his salary as possible. But he was a man of experience and knew that the raw material, added to the cost of running the plant, and the Pay Roll, would put any House out of business that had to meet stiff competition.

Late in September, James Barton was injured by a flying, broken belt. As usual, he had clambered up one of the steep ladders to take a hand in some machine repairs. The men carried him home and for many days he lay in the great blue bed-room, babbling over old and tender memories, and it was whispered about the town that the doctors feared he would never rise again.

At this time they sent for Tom Barton. Tom was a strong, pushing young man, possessing all the qualities his father lacked. As the head man in the Western Branch of the great Harvester Trust, he was thoroughly informed upon the latest methods of modern Business.

"Why in the name of Common Sense," Tom remarked to himself, after he had been long enough in command to measure his men, "does the pater pay fifteen dollars a week to old men when he can get young ones for seven or eight—and the young men able to turn out twice the work at that!" Thereafter he began to tinker with the Pay Roll.

Elimination of the weak is the first principle of "good business" and Tom put it into operation for Barton, Mathews & Co. He thought the man who had not accumulated a competence by the time he had reached forty belonged in the Junk Pile, and he never missed an opportunity of sending him there.

So Tom pared down wages till by the first of the year, though the machines had been speeded up several notches and the new force of young men kept the wheels moving at a clipper pace, the Pay Roll was reduced to less than half its former size.

Another phase of the business pained Tom even more deeply than the swollen pay roll. He learned that the standard of excellence his father and Sid Mathews had established during the early period of their manufacturing career, had been firmly maintained, or improved throughout the long years of the business life. Try as he did, Tom was unable to find where an inferior grade had been substituted either in the raw materials or in the finished products, themselves. Only perfect fixtures, fittings and machines went through that factory door. The smallest flaw never got past Jim Barton's honest inspection. But Tom inaugurated a new regime! It was well, he thought to begin making the Best Grade. This was the way to gain a reputation, but it was worse than a waste of money and effort for a firm to continue to improve its products. The value in a reputation-for-making-good-grade lay in the possibilites it afforded one for selling goods of an INFERIOR quality.

Under the new management, the company was able to shade its prices down to meet those of all competitors, while their old reputation for quality enabled them to gather in the orders.

Business picked up steadily and before long orders were booked three months ahead. But there were so many changes everywhere that when old Jim Barton drove down to the Plant one day he scarcely knew his own factory. The shock was so great that he suffered a relapse. After that he left things in Tom's hands.

The stockholders of the company were grieved at the first of the year to learn Barton, Mathews & Company would declare no dividends. Several of them grumbled, but Tom steered a steady course. He knew his own mind. When a man controls 51 per cent of the stock, it is more sensible to double his own salary and the salary of his friends than it is to pay dividends. When he thought of the 20 per cent the House had paid regularly year in and year out in the past, he wondered that the Business had not long before gone to the wall.

He wiped Sid Mathews' name off the "Charity" or "Pension List" and voted himself a salary of $10,000 a year.

Last spring Tom Barton married the daughter of the leading banker in Joplin, and—from all the Dun and Bradstreet reports—the young people are likely to live happily ever after.

Skinny's Turkey Dinner

Two weeks before Thanksgiving Day every newspaper in Chicago began to tell about it. Mr. H. Harrison Browne, they said, President of Browne, Johnson & Company, one of the largest wholesale grocery houses in the city, would give away, on the day before Thanksgiving, a carload of choice country turkeys.

The amount of free advertising Browne, Johnson & Company, and Mr. Browne in particular, received upon the strength of this bare announcement is almost incredible. Every branch of every charity bureau in the city received requests from him for the names of families particularly "worthy" to share Mr. Browne's bounty. Several ministers mentioned his name in writing their Thanksgiving sermons as a man of wealth for other rich men to emulate and for the poor to thank God for.

All over the city people were asking each other, how many good sized turkeys go to make up a car-load and everybody declared it was really very handsome of Browne, Johnson & Company, with turkeys at 27 cents a pound. It would be a good thing, they declared, if he could shame the Beef Trust into being reasonable for once, instead of holding everybody up during the holiday season.

The city papers gave columns lauding President Browne, and a sympathetic cub-reporter spent several evenings among the hard-working, underfed people on the West Side, gathering local color for a Thanksgiving story on Browne's Turkey Dinners.

And fully ten thousand underfed families read about Browne's carload of turkeys, and doubted and longed for one of them. The charity organizations were besieged with requests and pleas for notes of recommendation to the Browne Distributing Committee and the subject of universal interest in Packingtown, Bubbly Creek and all along Halsted street was Browne's free Thanksgiving turkeys.

Now Skinny McCarty was one of the scrappiest boys for his age, in Bubbly Creek, and he made up his mind to secure one of these free turkeys for the McCarty Thanksgiving dinner. His father, Dan McCarty, had been working on half time for so many months that the family well knew it was their only chance.

Skinny read all the papers and gathered sufficient information to know that the best way to secure one of the prizes would be to have a note from the Charity People. And, as Big Dan McCarty said, "Skinny was a bye with a turrible nerve." So to the Charity People he went. From past experience he realized that Miss Thompson, the investigator in whose territory he lived, would be the most likely person to approach.

Miss Thompson had long been prejudiced in Skinny's favor. When Dan McCarty had been laid off at the time of the advent of the last new McCarty baby she had found Skinny eager to get a paper route down town and to go into business. All the McCartys were cheerful, hard

International Socialist Review 10 (November 1909): 385–91.

working, and, as a rule, self-supporting. She believed in encouraging them.

So when Skinny explained about the "free turkeys" and asked for a note to Browne's Distributing Committee, he got it. Three times he was compelled to kick his feet waiting for Miss Thompson in the Bureau Investigating Room, but the morning before Thanksgiving Day his patience was rewarded and he returned to Bubbly Creek the envy of every boy and girl along the Alley.

Five minutes before he reached home, Mrs. McCarty, bending over her wash-tub, heard his triumphant shrill whistle and the smaller Mc-Cartys began to expand into the largest grins of which they were capable as they flew to meet Skinny.

This was the morning before Thanksgiving Day. The turkeys were to be given away from Browne, Johnson & Company's downtown wholesale store at four o'clock in the afternoon. So Skinny assumed an air of great importance, ate a slab of bread spread with fryings, and departed for the scene of his hopes.

His mother gave him a nickel to take the car home, for it was over five miles to Browne, Johnson & Company's store, and she hoped the turkey would be a heavy one. Besides it was not always safe for a small inhabitant of Bubbly Creek to parade his worldly wealth too freely without possessing the strength of arm necessary to protect it.

As Skinny strutted proudly down the Alley, Mrs. McCarty took her hands from the tub and stood watching him from the basement steps and bragged a little to Mrs. Smith, who lived next door, and thanked God for giving her such a smart "bye."

It was a long and interesting walk for Skinny down to Browne's and he enjoyed every step of it. He reveled too in the great masses of people that packed State street for nearly a block and swelled over and blocked the cars on Randolph. All these people had come hoping to get a free turkey too, but few of them would have notes from the Charity People. And his boy heart swelled with the pride of his own cleverness.

Long before three o'clock the crowd had become an impact mass through which it refused to allow newcomers to pass. But Skinny had, long before, slowly and laboriously wormed his way near the side door, where the papers said the Browne Distributing Committee would give out the turkeys. And still the people came till the whole street looked like a hive dotted and swarming with bees. At last Browne, Johnson & Company sent a call to the Police Department and a little later a squad arrived to clear the streets and disperse the crowd.

Skinny managed to hold his position near the big doors, and when the Distributing Committee finally made its appearance he shrilled instantly.

"I've got a letter from the Charity People; read it. They told me to give it to you an' you'd give me a turkey. Her name's Miss Thompson," and he frantically climbed over the rude platform and thrust the note into a man's hand. So Skinny was one of the first to receive a turkey.

With a deep sigh of joy, he threw it over his shoulder, holding firmly to its legs. Then he backed cautiously against the walls of the building. The air was very cold, but Skinny heeded it not, and when a few belated policemen appeared driving the crowd before their clubs, he followed at their backs, out of the crowd, and made his way to a South Side car.

As it leaked out afterward (though it did not leak far) only five hundred turkeys were really given away, but Skinny never knew that, and if he had known, he would have considered himself more lucky in securing one.

It was seven o'clock when he arrived home. Supper was on the table and a roaring fire in the stove, and the beaming smiles of his mother and the smaller McCarty's sent Skinny's spirits skyward in an ecstacy of pride and joy.

The turkey was hung on a nail outside the window, in the cold, but in full view from within. And Skinny persuaded Tim to sit in his place at the table so that he would not be compelled to tear his eyes from the lovely sight.

At eight o'clock came Dan McCarty home to dinner. Often it is not enough that a man shall work on "half time" but he must need work over hours to get out the job the boss wants done. So it was with Dan, but the smiling face of his wife and the grins on the faces of the children told him, at once, that Skinny had secured a turkey.

"Well, Bye," he said, after he had soused his face in the tin basin at the sink, and seated himself at the table, "I'm sure glad you got it."

"You'll sure be a success in loife, if you kape on gittin' things you wants, loike you do now."

And proud and very red face in the face, Skinny brought the treasure into the kitchen that the whole family, and his father in particular, might feel the heft of it and admire his smartness. Never in all his eleven years had Skinny accomplished a feat like this.

While Dan ate his supper, Mrs. McCarty sat beside him and the little McCartys chattered while Skinny walked about, alone, too big to play with the children (in the light of the day's work) and not old enough to sit beside his father. But all the joy and pride of a first success were his.

But the fire grew hot and Mrs. McCarty arose and began to clear off the dishes, as Dan wiped his mouth on the back of his hand and reached for his pipe.

"There's a turrible smell in here, Mary," he said, as he sniffed with his head in the air, while he filled it.

"There's sure somethin' dead in this kitchen, an' be the smell of it, I'd say it'd been dead a LONG time."

"Perhaps it's a rat," suggested Mrs. McCarty, while the children looked under the stove and poked behind the coal box. But there was no need to search long, for the heat from the kitchen stove had thawed the frozen treasure and an unmistakable odor of decayed flesh arose from the sink. Alas for the hope and faith we may have had in the philanthropy of the large advertiser! They are on the way to a severe setback, for the turkey—Skinny's prize turkey—was bad beyond the hope of eating on that Thanksgiving Day.

We cannot tell the history of that fowl, whether his days had been many or whether they were few, we only know—for Browne explained to the Charity Organizations afterward, that he had been "shamelessly cheated by the packing company." They had unloaded a lot of spoiled fowls upon him, taking advantage of his confidence and sent a number of turkeys spoiled in a wreck the previous summer on the T. and P. R. R., between Joplin, Mo., and Kansas City.

But Skinny was very young and full of hope. He refused to believe the evidence of his senses.

"All turkeys smell that way," he declared at first, and it was only when his father had forcibly separated him from the prize he thought he had won, that the truth penetrated his brain and the iron entered his soul. His mother said the turkey was bad; the other children said it SMELLED bad; and his father insisted,

"It was turrible ROTTEN."

So it was, that amid a storm of tears and with deep regret, that Dan McCarty deposited the turkey in that portion of the Alley where the scavengers are supposed to remove refuse, and Skinny McCarty's first illusion was destroyed.

He went to bed crying and fell asleep with the tears still wet on his cheeks, while Big Dan and his wife talked it over, and sighed and wondered if they couldn't afford a turkey dinner after all.

"We might," said Mrs. McCarty in despair, at last, "We MIGHT get a RABBIT." But just then BIG Dan thought of a way.

At two o'clock on Thanksgiving Day, garbed in their very best, Dan McCarty, his wife on his arm, and all the children began their long walk to Halsted street. With their free hands, Dan and Mary clutched the fists of Mamie and little Pete and kept them from falling over themselves. Kate piloted Buddie, and Skinny marched proudly before with a wary eye on Nick. For the moment, the tragedy of yesterday was forgotten by Skinny, in the joy of a new pair of shoes.

"You shall all have TURKEY for dinner," Big Dan had declared and Big Dan meant it. So the kiddies squirmed around and galloped along risking their own limbs and the equilibrium of their fond parents.

At Mike's Place they all spilled noisily into the Family Entrance, and such a squeaking of chairs and pushing of tables there was that Mike himself stuck his head through the swinging doors to see what the trouble was.

"Well, well," he said heartily, looking from one expectant face to another, "If it ain't Big Dan McCarty," and he nodded to Mrs. McCarty and mussed the childrens' hair.

"Mill runnin' on full time yet?" asked Mike. Big Dan said, "No, 'bout half toime," and ordered three beers, "an' a little of that Free Lunch for the kids."

"SURE!" Mike said, and disappeared through the swinging doors. He stayed so long that Dan began to fear he had forgotten the order, when the bar-keep's helper appeared staggering beneath a load that caused the small McCartys to squirm off their seats with joy!

For the helper bore a huge tray and upon that tray were there many plates, piled high with good things. Turkey there was—a whole leg for each one of the children, and mashed potatoes, pickles, bread and butter and cranberry sauce!

Then began such a clatter of knives and forks and such a smacking of lips as would drive a hungry man green with envy.

When the last crumb had been forced downward and Mrs. McCarty had straightened Tim's tie, and washed Buddie's face and hands and rebuttoned Katy's dress, Dan permitted Mamie to press the button. A moment later Mike's red face appeared.

"Won't you come in and have a drink with us?" Big Dan asked.

"It was sure a swell feed you're handin' out today." "Purty fair grub," Mike nodded. "No," he shook his head, and waved aside the money Big Dan had laid on the table.

"You're money ain't good here TO-DAY. What'll-it-be?"

"Beer," said Big Dan; "beer," said Mrs. McCarty, and Mike once more disappeared behind the swinging doors.

"Gee!" said Big Dan leaning toward Mary. "Mike's a hell-of-a foine fellow!"

Out of the Dump

One morning, ten years ago, when I was a little snip of a girl, Dad kissed us all goodbye, from mother down to the baby, and went off to work as usual. He never came back. It was this way. The third floor chute

International Socialist Review 8 (May 1908): 670–75; (June 1908): 746–51; 9 (October 1908): 266–71.

from the Can to the Canning Rooms down at the yards, had begun to give way and father was the first man sent over with a load, after one of the braces had been knocked out. He told the foreman how shaky the beams were, but that's as far as it went. Two of the men working near him told mother about it afterwards. But mother says one reason Dad held his job with the company so long was because he never backed away from risky jobs; nor kicked for safety appliances; nor harped on unsanitary conditions. I suppose that's why he didn't balk when it came to wheeling a great load over that broken chute.

He was always game, Dad was. Not at fighting the boss but game in the face of flying belts and broken machinery and death and disease and doing what the other men were afraid to do. He had been at Carton's for fifteen years, so perhaps that's why he didn't pit his staying qualities against the packing company. Fifteen years is long enough to make most anybody knuckle, especially when it's to the man who hands out the life-saving pay envelope every Saturday night.

Well, father was game once too often, for the beams supporting the old chute gave way and threw him head first into the yard. His spine was injured and the packing house doctor hustled him off in a delivery wagon to a hospital where the company (philanthropically?) supported a private ward. The House Attorney did what he was there for and kept his stenographer busy writing out affidavits which the canning floor workers were required to sign, showing how the accident had occurred through Daddy's own carelessness and the company wasn't to blame at all.

The same men that signed these papers came over to tell mother about the accident. You couldn't blame them for signing. It doesn't help much for two or three men to line up against the boss. They'd only be "laid off." It takes numbers to gain anything that way.

They wouldn't let mother see father when she applied for admission at the hospital. She cried and begged but they told her he would get along nicely if he was not disturbed. But the packing house lawyer was admitted at once. You see, it paid the hospital authorities to stand in with the packers. And it paid the Carton Packing Company to keep their attorney at father's side to get a statement from Daddy that would free them from liability. Nobody can accuse them of not looking after their own interests.

Perhaps, if his friends had been able to reach father's bedside, mother might have gotten a few thousand dollars damages from the packing company, and we children could been sent to school, which would have equipped us to bring better returns when we were put on the labor market later on. But if is a big word. Nobody saw father during his last moments but the callous packing house lawyer who brought away a paper which he claimed father signed, releasing the company from liability.

Life was very different for us all after that. Before the accident we had been tolerably sure of the two rooms over Mike's saloon which we called Home. And there was always bread and potatoes and sometimes soup and a stew for dinner. Mother had managed to send Bob and me and Katie and Tim to school a part of the time at least.

But after Dad went, life was a regular Lottery and a good many days were blanks. Mother took in so many washings for awhile that the walls of the basement room turned green with mold. But the Undertaker with his bill camped on her trail. . . .

At last, of course, the little mother gave up. She had worked several days in the steam filled room with a pain in her chest that kept her face white and drawn, but when the fever came on, she was forced to lie down on the old bed. When she found she was unable to rise, she said over and over again to herself.

"The babies, the babies! O my poor little babies! What can I do!" I made her a cup of tea; fed the younger children and put them to bed.

In the night mother was delirious. She woke me calling for somebody to look after Sammie and screaming for them not to take us away from her. She said she "would soon be able to work again." I ran up stairs and woke Mrs. Nome. Mrs. Nome was a lame old woman who sold shoe strings at the "L" Station. Often she'd send Bobbie to "Mike's" for a can of beer and the Flynns said she got tipsy and went to sleep on the stairs. I don't know about that. But she was very good to us.

When I told her mother was sick, she hopped down stairs and took charge. It was time somebody did. She was kind to mother for a long time. She didn't wash often; that's true, and she didn't believe in manicurists of any kind. She'd have "lifted" a watch from a rich man with her right hand, and spent the proceeds on us kiddies with her left, and been proud of it. That's the kind of a woman she was.

Mrs. Nome was almost as poor as we were. She couldn't feed five hungry waifs, nurse the mother and sell shoe strings. But she stuck to the little mother and assumed command. The wood was nearly gone; the rent was due and we had nothing to eat in the room, but Mrs. Nome was a woman of resources. Since she couldn't feed and warm us herself, she used the materials at hand. She just wrapped me up in a shawl and put one of Bob's old coats on little Sammie and hustled us up to a corner on the boulevard to beg.

We were hungry, Sammie and I, and all the other children were hungry too. Mrs. Nome chose to send Sammie because he was such a pale, wee little imp she thought nobody could turn him down. She said nobody but a "Charity woman" would do it. I know now that she meant the "Scientific Charity Worker" who is hired to nose around the shacks of the poor, hunting for evidence that will enable the charity officials to prounounce the verdict unworthy, from which there is no Appeal, upon the miserable ones. . . .

"Don't never let them Charity people know where ye live," she said, "Er they'll be down en takin' all you kiddies away from yer maw en sendin' ye to the 'Friendless.' Tell 'em yer name's Jones, Mary Jones, en thet ye live in the Alley. Don't never say nothin' about the Dump." . . .

Mrs. Nome was always worried with fear of the Charity Organization Society. It seems they'd have shoved her into the poor house long before had it not been for the inevitable shoe strings which she hawked. They could never catch her asleep. Always she patently vended her small wares. As there was nobody to prove she didn't earn her own living it was impossible to chuck her away on the County and she remained a lasting eyesore to "Scientific Charity."

Every outcast on the Dump was her ally and she served us all unaccountable good turns. Equally true were the Rich her bane and her abomination. And unbelievable too were the many small ways she found to beat them.

The days passed and she stuck to the helm of the Piper household, nursing the little mother through long nights of pain and feeding us children like a henmother come into her own. The rent was paid; we children were clothed and mother was supplied with medicine. . . .

But all good things come to an end. Sammie and I met our finish when we ran into Charles K. Copperthwaite, Superintendent of the Board of Organized Charities. A smug Board of Trade man had just given us a quarter and was hurrying away when up comes Old Copperthwaite. It was the very end. I had six dollars in my pocket when he started out to take us home and "investigate." . . .

. . . [He] turned on the flashlights and wrote us up in the papers. He roasted the people who had given us money instead of paying it to the Charity Organizations for "investigating" us, and he boosted his own particular organization way up and over. He proved that we had eight dollars in cash in the basement when Sammie and I went out to "impose on a noble-hearted but careless-minded Public."

And then he sent Katie and Tim to the Home for the Friendless and persuaded Mrs. Chauncey Van Kleeck to take me into "her beautiful home" as a watch-dog for her baby, for my board, clothes and schooling. You can go into the Office of the Bureau to this day and read how "charitable" Mrs. Van. was; and see the notes she sent in to the officers every month reporting the moral progress and ability to work shown by the little "beggar."

Copperthwaite got all the philanthropically inclined society ladies to "take such an interest" in mother that before she could raise her head off her pillow, she was nearly smothered with family washings—which the dear ladies sent her out of the kindness of their hearts—at half the rates usually paid for such work. "It will enable her," said Copperthwaithe in the papers, "to maintain an honest living and keep the two younger children at home." Then he painted a halo around the head of the financially elect, and I suppose the society ladies glowed with virtue when they read the papers, thinking they saw themselves as others see them. . . .

I was eleven when I went to live with the Van Kleecks nine years ago, and for several months I felt that I was in a fairy land. . . .

I had never imagined dresses of such exquisite texture, nor china so rare, nor real gold plate anywhere outside of Grimm's Fairy Tales. In the great house, surrounded by the grounds filled with stately trees, I was happy for a time to be an unmarked observer of the life of the Leisure Class. Mrs. Van Kleeck was usually so overwhelmed with receptions, musicals, balls or dinners that she forgot all about me until she was called upon for her quarterly report from the Home Finding Department of the Charity Organization Society.

In all my life I had never known people who could afford to satisfy their desires, and the Van Kleecks had only to want and be filled. It was to me a new order of things to hear little Holly Van Kleeck, aged six, demand a new pony and English cart, ANOTHER miniature automobile or a small duplicate of his father's Swiss watch set with diamonds, or some other inconceivable extravagance, and everybody running around to satisfy his demands. I pinched myself when I saw him bang the same watch over his tutor's head and break it. The whole world seemed turned upside down.

But money was nothing at all to the Van Kleecks. Holly had a dog harness for his bull terrier, pegged with knobs of beaten brass, that cost more than a year's rent down at the Dump. And his father roared with laughter when Holly threw it into the blazing fire during an evening romp.

It struck me with continual wonder, that first year, to see lap robes, the price of which would have fed the Higgenses royally for a whole year. I was dumb before a homely red vase that was worth money enough to have saved Pete Miller's leg when it was crushed by the street car, and amputated a few days later on account of unskillful treatment. It was unbelievable that any woman should spend enough money on a single gown to have bought a house and lot in the Alley.

The maid in the left wing enjoyed telling me about these things for I sat mouth agape drinking in the new wonders like a young gourmand, or sat stunned trying to understand that there really was as much money in the world as the Van Kleecks seemed to possess. I had always had grave doubts upon the matter before. Indeed, I was too amazed trying to assimilate these new standards to feel much loneliness. It was a glorious and continuous fairyland performance and I only awoke after six or seven months of it. . . .

When I went to work at the office of the Charity Organization Society, the first thing I noticed was a great sign placed over the door through which the "applicants" are obliged to pass when they want to ask for help. It reads this way: "ALL THINGS COME TO THOSE WHO WORK." I thought of Mrs. Van Kleeck and I laughed inwardly for many days whenever I saw that sign.

Mr. and Mrs. Van Kleeck and the friends in their set were liberal givers to all the charity organizations, and scarcely a day passed that an employee from the Van Kleeck stores or factory did not apply to one of the organizations for help of some kind. Five dollars a week was the average wage paid to clerks, and you can't make that amount stretch over seven days, try as you may. Besides, the girls are required to dress well and the shabby girl will not be kept long. When a girl is trying to support her mother, or her brother and sisters on five or six dollars a week, she is pretty certain to need aid from somebody very soon. So the Emporium came to be known as The School for Scandal and many of the girls were forced to add to this pittance in another way.

It was unbearably humiliating applying at the charity societies and if you needed a new and decent waist to wear at the new job at Van Kleeck's in the morning it would be a pretty safe bet to lay on the fact that the whole family would be dead of starvation before the "Scientific" Investigators got down to a working basis. Or they might present you with an antediluvian waist that The School for Scandal wouldn't employ at the wrapping counter.

They will tell you, at the charity organizations, that Hollister Van Kleeck, Jr., gave a thousand dollars one year to The Home for Delinquent Females and that Mrs. Van Kleeck became so much interested in the work of checking the social evil that she put up enough money to publish a book on the subject written by one of the "Charity experts."

There was not, however, any mention made in this book of The School for Scandal; nor was there in it anywhere a hint of a real cure for the disease.

The Right Reverend Doctor Squab tells us that religion will remove the cause; that when the heart is "purified" women will no longer "desire to sell themselves!" As though any man or woman ever wished to sell themselves—in any way!

The purpose of Scientific Charity is to provide the members of a family with work paying enough to enable them to live, and if a hundred thousand men or women in any of our large cities should stop work tomorrow, there would be more men and women than would be needed applying to fill those positions the next day. When there are two girls for every job, you can't get jobs for all of us. So it is impossible for the most "scientific" Charity organizations to be "scientific" much of the time.

When a "Scientific" Investigator had Kate Miller's case in hand, Katy was working at the ribbon counter in the Van Kleeck downtown retail store. She was trying to support her mother and herself on five dollars a week, when one of the buyers took a fancy to her. He paid the room rent and bought her a new dress before he went to New York. Things got worse for Katy after that, instead of better, till the "Scientific" Investigator got hold of her. She lectured Kate and advised her to get a room with some family that would permit her to work at night for her board. Then she brought some sewing for Mrs. Miller, which she was unable to do, with her hands all pinched up from rheumatism. Katy would not go out to work evenings, because she knew somebody had to be home to look after her mother, but they moved into a cheaper room, which the Investigator found and which was so far away from the store that Katy had to pay car fare to the store or walk four miles night and morning.

Then the Investigator fussed with Katy for a while and wanted her to put her mother in The Old Folks' Home, where Katy could support her comfortably by paying only a dollar a week. Katy finally consented, but the Investigator found that Mrs. Miller was six months below the required sixty-five years of age, or not an American-born, or that she was a Catholic, or there was no vacancy or some other unconquerable obstacle—it may have been she had not been a resident of the state over ten years—I can't remember what it was; anyway they found Katy would have to go on supporting her mother the same as ever.

About that time the Investigator got busy on another case, but she did not neglect the Miller family. She sent down a bag of beans and some salt pork, and called around to see how they were doing about two weeks later.

In the meantime the new landlady insisted on having the room rent when it came due. Katy kept right on in the new way till Mrs. Deneen gave them notice and then she made up her mind there was nothing in reforming.

The Investigator was disgusted when the neighbors told her about the Millers and the Society gave Katy up as a bad lot and marked "Very immoral; don't seem to want to do right; UNDESERVING" after her name on the books. It would have done Katy no good to apply there for help after that. . . .

John Copperthwaite was the hardest, least sympathetic man I have ever known. He cared nothing at all about the Poor. His chief ambition was to become the highest salaried man working in the field wherein he shone. He was one of the fathers of "Scientific Charity" and desired to be quoted upon all philanthropic questions as the greatest American authority upon the subject.

His motto was "Teach the Poor self-help." It was very simple. All the investigator had to do was to advise the applicant to "get work." According to old Copperthwaite, every time an organization GAVE anything to a poor man or woman that organization proved itself inefficient. He believed that a perfect institution should pay next to nothing in practical aid—or "relief," as he called it. He said he hoped to live to see the time when charity workers would be educated to the point where they would realize the importance of spending 99 percent of all money received for the Cause in the "Scientific Way." The investigators would be educated workers. They would be able to promptly separate the many "unworthy" from the "worthy" poor. Of course it did not matter what became of the "unworthies." The "worthy" ones would appeal to the investigators; drink in a little Wisdom on How to Help Themselves and go upon their ways rejoicing.

But I do not mean to discuss the uncharitable charity workers, nor the dishonest ones. There are uncharitable and dishonest people everywhere. Rather I wish to tell about those whose greatest joy is in aiding and helping the poor and unfortunate. It concerns us only whether THEY are able to cope with the great and INCREASING illness—Poverty.

Fortunately Mr. Copperthwaite decided to send me over to assist in the office of Mr. Pythias. And he was truly a friend—a Pythian, to the poor as far as in his power lay.

His eyes filled with tears when I told him about mother and Bob and my wish to make a little home for Sam and Maggie.

"Well, well, well!" he said sympathetically. "We'll see if we can't manage it."

And so he installed me in the great store rooms and before long I was busy clothing the naked Poor in the cast-off garments of the Rich. Mr. Pythias paid me seven dollars a week besides giving me some good warm clothes for Sam and Maggie. Our rent was $2.00 a week. And Mrs. Maloney, who lived just overhead, kept an eye on the children every day till I came home.

In a short time they had learned to put the potatoes to boil and to set the table before I returned. We were really managing to get along very well. My work in the store rooms was always interesting and I found the winter days slipping away faster than I had dreamed possible. I was too busy to feel very lonely. The housework had to be accomplished in the evenings and Sam and Maggie were beginning to take pleasure in making things "look nice."

As I said before my work in the store rooms of the Northwest Bureau grew more interesting every day. The greatest desire of Mr. Pythias's heart was to help the Poor and he inspired all his workers with zeal in this direction. He wished too to help them permanently, to put them on the road to happy, wholesome, self-supporting lives. But this was impossible except in a very few cases. I have seen him sit at his desk with his great head bowed in his hands and doubt and perplexity filling his heart. He reminded me of the physician who puts salve on the sore he fears will never heal; the physician who knows that his efforts may assuage the pain but can never CURE the disease.

During those days it seems to me I was absorbing views of Charity Work at every pore and from a dozen angles. I talked with the investigators and with the applicants. I read the reports made out on the various cases. I studied books by representative charity workers. Better still, I had not lived seven years in the home of the Van Kleecks without acquiring a tolerable knowledge of the lives of the rich patrons of the various organizations. It's easier to learn about their inside phases in the Servants' Quarters than it is from the drawing rooms. And what I don't know about the people from The Alley, The Dump or Bubbley Creek isn't worth putting down on the records. You see, I'm ONE OF THEM. So when I saw a motto over the mahogany desk of Mr. Copperthwaite that read:

"Not MONEY but ENCOURAGEMENT is what the Poor need"—Leo Tolstoi,

I knew it was in the Upper Element where Stupidity reigned supreme. Anybody who looks over the records of the various cases can see that either directly or indirectly the cause of distress in ninety-five cases out of one hundred is LACK of EMPLOYMENT or INSUFFICIENT INCOME. Over 65 percent were so reported by the investigators. But in a case like the one of John Walters, where the man deserted his wife and children because he was unable to get work and because he knew it was the only way to secure aid for them from the charity organizations, the *apparent* cause of distress is DESERTION.

Although so reported by the charity investigator, it was not because of SICKNESS that the Wineshevsky family was in need. Neither they, nor the thousands of other families that are dying every year in unhealthy tenements or unsanitary houses, choose to live in them. They love sunshine and fresh air and beautiful homes as well as anybody. But a poor wage worker has to take what he can get. And so the babies die year after year.

Rip Mahoney hadn't been a drunkard BEFORE he was injured and his family was not sinking into the hopeless mire of misery because of his drunkenness. Rip drank BECAUSE he WAS rendered hopeless, because he was unable to keep his family FROM SINKING. Of course he was unable to get anything from the street railway company when his back was hurt. He couldn't afford a lawyer. You might say he was "improvident" because he had never been able to save anything out of his enormous salary of nine dollars a week.

I saw very clearly before I had worked very long for Mr. Pythias, that the disease that was killing my people was Poverty, lack-of-work, and I longed to find a cure in the name of the thousands of miserable ones. . . .

My next visitor was O. Carrington Lee. Mr. Pythias brought him up, introduced us in his kindly manner and returned to his office. Mr. Lee explained that his man was bringing a lot of things which Mr. Lee wanted to donate. And the "man" shortly appeared heavily laden with clothing. There were twenty of Mr. Lee's "old suits" (as good as new) in the lot. Ten of them were of the finest linen, for Mr. Lee had wintered at Tampa, Fla. And there were fourteen fancy vests, silken hose and underwear, half a cart-load of shoes and nearly two dozen fine shirts.

I knew a great deal about Mr. Lee. Mr. Pythias was fond of talking about this man, who, in spite of his great wealth and social position, still had time and money to spend upon those who were less fortunate than he.

He was very good to look at, one of those tall, hardy, well-groomed young men who have all their lives fed upon the Cream of things; a clean-limbed, frank and noble young man who has had all those riches and pleasures handed to him that poor folks are forced to make themselves "ignoble" to secure.

He glanced around the great room with the same quick and interested manner Bob has. And my heart pounded hotly and my eyes grew moist. He was what Bob might have been if OUR father had left us two or three business blocks when HE died. Poor Bob! who was spending his young days in the House of Correction because he was forced to stealing in order to take care of mother! I looked at Mr. Lee's hands. O yes! All his fingers were there. He had never worked at a "lapping machine." Probably his father had left him the OWNER of one.

Mr. Lee walked about the store room with an assured step as though he had a right to be there.

"I want you to see, Miss Piper," he said pleasantly, "that the things I have brought over are given to WORTHY people."

"I don't understand, Mr. Lee," I said quickly, for I felt that I would choke in my wrath. He looked up surprised.

"Worthy, DESERVING," he repeated. "You understand."

"No, but I DON'T understand," I repeated. "Is there any one who is 'unworthy'?"

"But the LAZY men, the DRUNKEN men, the DISHONEST men. I mean them, of course," he said. And I must confess that he spoke kindly and earnestly. The rage and anger died out of my heart for I thought, if Bob had been born in his bed he would have been just such a strong, handsome, stupid young man. It wasn't Mr. Lee's fault that he did not know our lives. But it seemed to me then that he was our enemy for all that; that the reason he, and such men as he, might live prodigally all their lives was because we poor folks slaved ourselves to death for a pittance. But I felt weary of a sudden. We were too far apart. I could never make him understand. It seemed useless to try. I thought I would not.

Mr. Lee kept his eyes upon me. He was waiting for an answer. And I smiled a little, though my eyes were wet.

"You see, Mr. Lee," I said, "I was born in The Dump. I've lived there most of my life. I'm one of those people. I know and come from the folks some of whom you call 'unworthy.'"

"I have a brother eighteen years old in the House of Correction. YOU would call him a criminal. He stole, I believe, in order to get money to save my mother when she was dying.

"He is younger than you. He has had scarcely any schooling, but he is a great deal smarter than you are.

"When our father was killed he left a debt which Bob worked one year to pay. He was twelve years old. He has been working almost ever since. Your father left you a great deal of valuable property. That's the only difference between you."

Just then one of the Mahoney children came up stairs with an order for a pair of trousers and some underwear, and while I was waiting on him, and trying to choke back the tears, Mr. Lee slipped away. I hoped he would not be angry or tell Mr. Pythias that I had been rude, but I was glad I had spoken anyway.

Bob spoke the truth when he said the thing that was hardest to endure was the judgment of the people who have inherited Rector Meal tickets for life. The morality they preach is wholly impossible to the Poor. Through the devious and troubled pathways which we tread the fierce struggle for existence breaks down the barriers of refinement, of modesty, of virtue and of honesty. If we are not ever intent upon the main issue, we fall on the way. To secure is to live. Some one has said, "There is not living a very poor, *honest* man." I wonder if it is because the very poor, very honest people die young!

The capitalists love a moral working man. He is patriotic! He will fight then for his country! All the Kings of Industry have to do when their warehouses are crammed to the bursting point is to pick a quarrel with one of the little countries. Somebody insults the Flag! The dear old flag! And the moral, patriotic man is up in arms in a moment ready to shoot the little Cuban, or Mexican, or Venezuelan into the eternal darkness, or to be himself shot. And so the Beef Trust gets a new market and the cotton trust another lease on life.

But honesty and industry as well as thrift are the great bulwarks of capitalism. An honest man will take nothing from the Rich. No matter how the rich man secured his wealth the honest man will have none of it. He is honest. He goes down to his grave honest. But that does not matter to the capitalist. Workingmen are a glut on the market! Always there are many more begging for jobs!

And the industrious man! Is he not a valuable employee? Is his labor not more productive to the man who hires him?

And the thrifty one! Can he not work for lower wages? Does he not save and pinch and deny himself in good times against a Rainy Day? He does not need to ask for Charity and is it not the Rich who support charity.

Verily! Verily! It seems to me that the reward of Virtue and Morality in the workingman goes very surely into the pockets of the Rich! . . .

Stories of the Cave People

THE ORNAMENT OF BIG NOSE

As far back as any of the Cave People could remember, their fathers had used the bones of wild beasts as weapons. I suppose they discovered long before that the marrow inside these bones was very good to eat. Then they hammered them with great stones till the bones split open and after they had eaten the marrow somebody discovered the sharp bones made very formidable weapons. No one had ever found sticks so strong and so sharp as these bone weapons.

By and by all the Cave People possessed great bones, split at one end, like a sharp sword. Almost every day the youths and maidens threw bones or sticks to display their skill. And the one whose aim was true and who showed most power in his arm, strutted about and stuck out his chest, in order that all the other Cave People might know how great he was.

International Socialist Review 9 (May 1909): 845–51.

One there was whom they called Big Nose. Now in the time of the Cave People it was a marvelous thing for a child to possess a nose that protruded. Generally cave noses were much like the noses of the Tree People, with merely two large nostrils in the centre of the face, slightly extended, preceding the head in order that the owner might catch the smell of danger or of good food. But him the Cave People called Big Nose because his nose turned down instead of upward, and it extended nearly half an inch beyond his face.

When he was only a slim, brown youth, Big Nose became able to out-throw all the other young folks. He could fling his rough bone javelin many feet further than any of the others and with greater force. At the edge of the woods, he would hurl it far among the trees and clip off, every time, the heads of the small purple flower that grew tall and slim in the forest.

Big Nose grew proud and held his head very high. And he began, after a little while, to wander farther and farther into the woods alone, for he desired greatly to meet the mountain lion or the green snake, in order that he might kill them with his weapon and become still greater in the eyes of the Cave People.

Every one thought he was brave but very foolish, for the youths and maidens rarely wandered about in the forest alone. Too often had their brothers gone out and never returned, and there was fear in their hearts.

But in spite of their warnings, Big Nose continued to hunt and one day, when he had traveled beyond the great rocks, he discovered a large tree lying prone upon the ground. The spring storms had uprooted it and flung it down to die.

Big Nose sped on till he reached the oak tree, when he heard, from its branches, a deep growl and much scratching. Big Nose drew back quickly and sheltered himself behind a great tree, waiting. Aloft he held his bone spear, readly to hurl it upon the enemy.

He waited a long time but nothing came forth from the boughs of the oak tree and gradually he grew bolder and cautiously advanced again. His ears twitched constantly and he drew his lips back from his teeth just as dogs do when they attack the enemy.

Big Nose still heard the low growling but he saw nothing. When he reached the fallen oak, he saw that its branches were flung over a deep hole in the ground. He peered into it carefully and saw a black bear, digging frantically with her paws. Evidently she had blundered through the branches of the tree and had fallen down into the hollow.

When Big Nose found there was no danger, he grew very happy and laughed softly to himself, for the black bear stood upon her hind feet and clawed the air, trying to get out.

And he dropped stones upon her head till she grew wild with rage and staggered about trying to reach him with her paws. Big Nose laughed softly and continued to tease her, till she stood again on her hind feet, exposing her throat in rage. Then he lifted his arms above his head and flung the bone javelin into her breast with all his strength.

The bear dropped to the ground pawing at the bone which protruded from her throat, dripping with blood. Furiously she tore about the pit, beating its sides with her paws. And Big Nose was terrified when he saw his bone weapon fall to the bottom of the hollow, and he ran about hunting for a long stick with which he hoped to poke it out again.

When he returned to the pit, bearing sticks and boughs, he found the bear pressing her paws to her breast and growling with rage.

Very carefully he bent over the hollow and poked his weapon, but the bear discovered his movement and turned quickly upon him. With a stroke of her great paw, she slashed savagely at his arm, and laid it open to the bone. Big Nose choked back a cry of pain.

Then he arose to his feet and staggered homeward. Softly he went and his feet touched the earth gently. Dry leaves did not crack under them and he made no sound. But his wound bled badly and he grew weak with pain.

Then he stopped at the side of a dead tree and tore off a strip of bark, which he wrapped tightly around his arm. And he sped quickly, for wild beasts came forth eagerly at the smell of blood and he had no weapon with which to defend himself.

But he arrived at the Hollow in safety. And the old men among the Cave People nodded their heads and threw out their hands, as much as to say,

"We told you so."

But the youths and maidens gathered around Big Nose with much interest, saying "What? What?" which, in the language of the Cave People, means, What is the matter?

And the brown maidens came near and gazed upon Big Nose with wonder and admiration. Even Light Foot, who had, alone, slain the man, who came down the river, from the enemies, the Arrow People, was pleased with Big Nose and brought herbs with which to wrap his wounds.

But Big Nose waved them all aside with a lofty gesture. Though the pain hurt him sorely, his face was calm, and he knew all the Cave People would think long of his bravery. And his blood was warm because Light Foot looked upon him with love and fire in her eyes.

When all the eyes of the Cave People were directed upon him, Big Nose knelt quickly on the ground and dug a small hole in the earth. With his arm that was uninjured, he pointed into it, growling an imitation of the black bear. And they knew he had discovered a bear that had stumbled into a hollow. Then Big Nose threw a stick into the hole and they understood he had hurled his bone javelin upon the bear. Snatching a second stick, he poked furiously to show how he had sought to extricate his weapon. With another deep growl, he pulled out his arm and held his wound where all could see.

It was in this way that the Cave People talked to each other. Their words were few and most of their ideas were expressed by gestures. "Quack, quack," they said when they meant wild duck. A deep growl signified the black bear, while a long line, made by drawing a finger through the dust or sand, gave everybody to understand the person spoke of a snake.

If you have seen a pantomime show, you will understand something of the manner of the gesture language of the Cave People. Even we "civilized" folks, long accustomed to verbal language, say many things to each other, every day, by facial expression and by gesture.

And so, even the children among the Cave People understood the adventures Big Nose had encountered. When his pantomime monologue was finished, the men and women of the tribe rose eagerly. They pointed first to the hole Big Nose had dug in the ground, and then toward the forest, as much as to say,

"Is the bear still in the pit?"

And one of them asked "Big Nose kill?" Big Nose shook his head and started toward the wood, indicating that the Cave Men were to follow.

So the strong men started through the forest. They hurried forward, keeping close together with their bone javelins in their hands. For it was growing dusk. But all were hungry and Cave People, who have eaten little for twenty-four hours, are willing to risk some danger for a meal of fresh meat.

They reached the pit safely. The bear still growled savagely in pain and it was after much jabbing with their bone weapons that they dispatched her.

Speedily they dragged her from the hole and began at once to skin and disembowel her. They worked into the dark hacking up and distributing portions in order that each man might carry back to the Hollow, his share of the burden.

Very sharply the Cave Men drew in their breath for the fresh blood of the bear smelled good to them. But the terror of the night was strong upon them, and they listened intently, sniffing the air, twitching their ears and trembling with fear. For it is in the night that the wild beasts creep forth for food and the smell of fresh blood reaches a long way off.

So the Cave Men huddled together very close, each carrying a portion of the dripping carcass of the bear. Big Nose too, bore a huge chunk of the meat, which he chewed from time to time. His wounded arm ached sorely, but because of the pride in his heart, he spoke not. But the way to the Hollow seemed very far and his knees almost sank beneath him.

Each man bore his bone weapon pointing away from his fellows, in order that the hyena, if it sprang at them, might receive the sharp bone point.

Strong Arm was he who thought most of the fire and the safety it brought. But he was unable to express his thoughts. For the sign of the fire among the Cave People was spoken in a gesture, and gesture language is not understood in the darkness.

One terrifying incident marked the journey home. Soft foot-falls crumbled the leaves and two green eyes spotted the black, but the Cave Men huddled closer together, and shrieked so loudly that the animal, whatever it was, dashed away in fear.

When they came to the Hollow, the Cave Men called loudly to the others, and distributed big chunks of bear meat, which they all ate eagerly, with great satisfaction. Then the people crept into their caves, rolled great stones before the entrances, and slept.

Many suns came and went away again and Big Nose was so proud of his wound that he moved his arm with great care. The blood that covered it grew hard and black but he sought to preserve it there always, in order to recall to the minds of the Cave People thoughts of his courage. To him it was a precious ornament, so beautiful that it caused the young men to regard him with jealousy and the young women with admiration.

And Light Foot, who was very beautiful in the eyes of all the Cave People, refused to look any longer upon the other youths of the tribe. And when Big Nose asked her to share his cave, she was proud and happy and went to live with him and became his wife.

One there was among the youths of the Cave People, whom they had never called "Man," which was to say, "you are wise and brave; therefore you are a man." Him they called Run Fast, because, in spite of the hair grown heavy upon his face, it was always his custom to run away when trouble came.

All the Cave People were often afraid, for death sometimes lurked in the shadows, and their ignorance was so great that they were unable to explain very common occurrences. But Run Fast was more fearful than the old women and the little children.

Run Fast hated Big Nose because Big Nose had done all the things he was afraid to do.

But one day he crept into the wood. He thought he knew of a way that would cause all the Cave People to look upon him with admiration. He did not see Laughing Boy slip through the brush behind him.

Run Fast did not travel far. He never went far from the Hollow when he was alone. And he did not see little Laughing Boy who watched him curiously from the bushes.

Then Run Fast did a very strange thing. Seizing his split bone knife, he scraped his arm till the blood ran and dropped on the ground. Then he bound it tightly, with a piece of bark, just as Big Nose had done.

He returned to the Hollow, screaming wildly, until the Cave People gathered to learn the cause of his distress. And he repeated, in the language of gesture, the same story Big Nose had told a few suns before.

The strong men and the women surveyed him sharply for it did not seem possible to them that Run Fast had killed anything. But little Laughing Boy, who saw that Run Fast was receiving much attention because of the blood upon his arm, pushed his way among the people.

With a stone in his hand, he rubbed fiercely up and down his forearm, till the blood flowed, pointing to Run Fast and shaking his head.

His meaning was plain. The Cave People understood him. It was, "See me. I can scratch myself harder than Run Fast did."

Then all the Cave People knew what Run Fast had done and they cried "Baby! Baby!" to Run Fast and he was disgraced before them all.

After that, when the young men of the tribe came home with blood upon their bodies, the strong men shook their heads and refused to believe tales of their adventures, unless they brought back something to prove their words. So it came to be a custom among the Cave People that the men or women who had killed a savage beast carried home with him the tail, or the hide or teeth of that animal. These they wore always as tokens of their bravery. Thus the Cave People first adorned their bodies.

LITTLE LAUGHING BOY

When the luscious fruit ripened and fell and the nut season came around, the time of joy and plenty was at hand for the Cave Dwellers. Then millions of fish sought the shallows of the river; nourishing plants, with a strange bitter-sweet flavor, thrust up their heads, and the nests were full of eggs for the hand of him who cared to gather.

It was then only that the Cave People were never hungry. With plenty abounding always in the forest, they feasted continually and grew fat against those periods of famine that spread through the long aftersuns and the dreary wet seasons.

True it was, that their enemies of the forest throve and grew strong also. The green snakes awoke and wound themselves around the branches of trees, with eyes that glistened and glowed toward every

International Socialist Review 10 (July 1909): 23–31.

living creature. And the brush grew thick and abounded with creeping things.

The cubs of the black bear flourished and the fierce hyena yielded bounteously to her young. Great flocks of strange and familiar birds darkened the sky and swooped down upon the berry bushes and swept them bare. But for all these, there was enough and to spare for the wants of the Cave Dwellers.

Even the limbs of Strong Arm, the wise and brave, grew soft during this season, for his stomach was always filled. The fierce rays of the tropical sun beat down upon the heads of the Cave Dwellers, filling them with a sweet drowsiness. There was nothing to drive them forth from the shades of the Hollow, where the waters of the river washed the green rocks, and teemed with thousands of golden and silver fish.

It was not in the season of plenty that the Cave People learned new ways to trap the black bear, or to snare the wild pig. Nor did they at that time seek to fashion new weapons or to travel strange paths. Rarely they plied the waters. These were not the days of progress or discovery, and the minds of the Cave people grew torpid and they forgot many things they had learned in the times of hunger and activity.

The hands of the youths and maidens lost a portion of their cunning and the older members of the tribe grew lazy and dull. For the bread fruit ripened and the tubers grew thick and all the land smiled with a bountiful supply of daily food.

The season of plenty was come. And the Cave People loved and laughed and feasted and were content. Few dangers menaced during those days and the members of the tribe forgot their fears and drowsed in peace.

But the children of the Cave People grew strong, lifting their heads. The fierce rays of the sun were unable to subdue them. Laughing Boy, grown tall and straight, was weaned at last. Always he laughed, showing his large white teeth, like a dark dog snapping at a bone. And he danced and ran about, spilling the strong life that surged up within him and would not be stilled.

With his young friend, The Fish, whom the Cave People had given his name because of his early skill in swimming, Laughing Boy learned many things. Their joy and juvenility seemed exhaustless, and their romps and chatterings ended only with the days.

Not many years before, the fathers and mothers of the Cave People had come down out of the trees to dwell. The Tree Dwellers found shelter in the natural caves that lined the river bank. In time they learned to walk erect, on two legs. The Cave Dwellers resembled them very closely. The arms of the Cave people had grown shorter as they ceased to swing themselves constantly, from tree to tree. The thumb of the foot disappeared and they now possessed a great toe in its place. Still the feet of the Cave Dwellers retained the power of prehension. They were able to hold—to cling awkwardly with them.

In the children this power was very marked. On the skirts of the forest they loved to clamber up the slim trees, poise on the swaying boughs and swing themselves from branch to branch, like young monkeys. This gave them strength of limb and quickness of vision. Soon they learned to choose those branches strong enough to bear their weight, as they flung themselves great gaps of space to seize the boughs of a neighboring tree.

But the fear of the green snakes, that wound about and hid themselves among the leaves, kept them near the Hollow. Only on rare occasions did they penetrate deep into the forest.

Among many of the savages living today, great skill and agility prevails. We are told of tribes whose members are able, by a partial circling of the trunks, with their arms, and by clinging and pressing of flexible toes, to mount trees in a sort of walk.

Jack London writes that this is a common practice of the natives of the South Sea Islands. And we are assured by several young friends that the art has not wholly disappeared among our own boys.

Many were the feats accomplished among the swaying branches of the trees by Laughing Boy, and his friend, The Fish, in their frolics many years ago. Their feet were never still. Their jabberings flowed without end. Tireless as the birds they were and gay as youth itself.

One day, as they played, Laughing Boy found a flat, curved piece of wood. It was as long as the arm of a man and had been split from a tree during a storm. Laughing Boy hurled the stick far into the air at his friend, The Fish. But The Fish threw himself from the bank, into the river, to avoid it. And he screamed with joy, as he disappeared beneath the waters. Then a very strange thing happened. For the flat stick swished through the air, like a great bird, far over the river. Then it turned about and whirled slowly back again, where it fell at the feet of Laughing Boy. At once the hair of his head rose with fear, and he ran to his mother uttering shrill squeals of alarm. Quack Quack awoke from her sleep and snatched up a bone-weapon, for she thought one of the forest enemies had attacked Laughing Boy.

But he pointed only to the strange, curved stick and clung to her, in terror. All the while he jabbered wildly. Quack Quack desired to quiet his fear, so she flung the stick far out over the river, as he had done. . . . [T]he big stick swished through the air, turned about and whirled gently back, striking her arm. Then it fell at her feet.

Whereupon Laughing Boy screamed and ran into the Cave. Then a great fear assailed Quack Quack and she added her cries to his. And all the Cave People hurried to her side to learn the cause of so much trouble.

Again the strange stick was hurled toward the river and once more it returned. And all the Cave People marveled and were afraid. For they could not understand a stick that returned when it was thrown.

Strong Arm only was brave enough to touch it with his fingers. His face bore a strange wonder that such things could be possible to a mere stick. And he carried it to his cave where he hid it among the rocks, under the dead leaves.

But when the nuts were gone and the season of plenty had passed away, and there was need for the Cave people to hunt, he brought it forth again. After many seasons, a flat stick, curved in the manner of the one first found by Laughing Boy, came to be used as a weapon by the Cave People. . . .

After a time the alarm and excitement, caused by Laughing Boy's discovery of the first rude boomerang, died away. The strange stick no longer menaced them and the Cave People returned to their feasting and their slumbers. And Laughing Boy and his young friend, The Fish, resumed their play.

They chased each other up and down the Hollow or concealed themselves in the long grass that lined the river bank. At each discovery they tossed and rolled over and over again, like puppies, wild with the exuberance of young blood.

It was one of their great pleasures to lie chattering in the grass on the top of the river bank and roll, tumbling, down into the clear waters. Then, amid a great splashing and much laughter, to clamber out and up the slope again. Thus the children of the Cave Dwellers romped and grew strong, during the season of plenty, in the days of old.

One day it chanced that Laughing Boy stumbled over a large co-coanut, during his frolics with his young friend. He seized it in his arms and danced about, jabbering with glee, that his friend might know the treasure he had found.

In an instant The Fish was upon him, but Laughing Boy rolled over in the grass and bounded away, with squeals of delight. Then, for no reason in the world, save that the blood pounded riotously in his veins, he darted into the wood, bearing his prize.

The Fish followed, close on his heels, as Laughing Boy threw shrill mocking cries over his shoulder. The Fish gave answer with a whirling stone, while more mocking cries from Laughing Boy announced that his aim was bad. And, O, the fun of the chase through the deep woods! The rolicking laugh and the deep shouts of The Fish as they startled the birds from their nests in the old forest!

The brush grew thicker with every step and the trees locked branches more closely with their neighbors for want of room to stretch them freely toward the sun.

When he reached the tall lautania palm which marked the point beyond which it was unsafe for the children of the Cave People to go alone, Laughing Boy concealed himself in the brush. He thought to be able to elude his own brown playmate, and while The Fish sought him beyond the bunya-bunya, to dash backward, toward the Hollow.

In a moment came The Fish. But the deep breathing of Laughing Boy and a rustling of the bushes made known his hiding place. As his friend had parted the thicket, Laughing Boy had time only to crawl out on the opposite side and dart onward ere he was caught. A shout and a shrill chattering told his victory, and he disappeared again. The Fish grunted his displeasure, but he was not far behind.

In the tall bambusa Laughing Boy again hid himself and it was by the tripping of The Fish over a creeping vine, that he escaped. But his foot blundered on a cone from the bunya tree and the cocoanut slipped from his hands. The two boys threw themselves downward and rolled over each other in their eagerness to recover it.

The Fish gave a shout of joy and made away, holding the cocoanut above his head for Laughing Boy to see. A warm sweat covered their bodies and their bronze skins shone like burnished copper.

On and on they ran. Further and still further they plunged into the depths of the forest. They forgot the dangers that lurked there and the wise warnings of the Cave People. They forgot their playmate, Crooked Leg, who had wandered into the wood and vanished from the face of the Hollow. Fears they had none, only laughter and the joy of abundant youth!

All this time the grown members of the tribe of the Cave people slept securely in the cool of the hollow. Their protruding bellies told of continued eating and no one among them marked the absence of The Fish and Laughing Boy.

Thicker and more dark grew the forest which the boys penetrated. The way grew rough, and the tough vines trailing through the undergrowth often tripped them. Still they lunged forward with no thought of turning their faces toward the Hollow.

It was a crackling in the brush that warned them. The cocoanut rolled from the hands of The Fish and the boys crouched low together. No sound they made, save the breath in their throats which struggled to be free. Couchant, they strained their bodies into an attitude of listening. Came again a soft rustling in the thicket. This time nearer. And then— through the long bambusa, they saw the head and throat of a grey hyena.

For a moment they paused while the sweat froze on their brown skins.

Their lips drew back in a snarl of helpless rage. But the hyena covered the ground with great bounds, and they flung their arms about a tall sapling. Their breath burst from them in quick gasps, for they were near spent with running.

But they dug their toes into the rough bark and the strength of The Fish enabled him to speedily mount to the forked branches above. But many moments Laughing Boy clung half-way up the trunk of the tree, with the hyena snapping at his heels. At every leap so near she came, that he curled his feet up under his small body. The teeth of the hyena shone white and her eyes gleamed. A great fear paralyzed him. The Fish danced about on the limbs above, chattering wildly, till Laughing Boy gathered breath and courage to continue his way to safety.

There he sat, huddled among the leaves, close to The Fish and for a long time they gazed, quivering, at the enemy below. But a caution, wholly new, had come to them, and they scrambled into the branches of a neighboring banyan slowly and with care. Thence on through several trees that brought them nearer the homes of the Cave Dwellers. With much shivering they made their way, pausing often to mark the progress of the enemy. She moved as they advanced, persistently, like a hungry dog watching a bone.

Slowly and fearfully the boys continued toward the Hollow, through the interlocked limbs of the great trees. But the hyena followed. From a bunya-bunya the boys pelted her with cones, which she dodged easily. Unmoved, she continued to gaze longingly upon them, while the slather dripped from her lips.

At one time the boys almost threw themselves into the coils of a huge green snake, that wound itself around the trunk of a cocoanut palm. They were not expecting new dangers. A quick leap and they swung downward, clinging closely to the bough of a neighboring bunya, and they scrambled up to safety once more. Thus they made on, but the distance they had run so joyously a short time before, seemed now to stretch before them without end. Sometimes they paused to rest and gather breath. At these points they huddled together and whimpered very low, or snarled, jabbering at the enemy, as she sat on her haunches, waiting.

But the glad time came when they saw below the familiar berry bushes. Beyond that the arboreal way was not unknown. With a new freedom and ease they flung themselves forward. Their leaps grew daring and their feet more sure, till at last they reached the edge of the wood near the Hollow.

Here they lifted their voices in sharp cries that aroused the Cave People from their torpor. Soon the stalwart members of the tribe had seized their bone weapons and hurried to the rescue.

At first the hyena did not retreat before them, but darted in and out slashing the Cave People with great fangs. But the fierce stabs of many bone weapons soon sent her fleeing back into the forest. Soon Quack Quack soothed the whimpering of Laughing Boy, holding him close to her breast.

The nut seasons came and the nut seasons passed away and Laughing Boy grew tall and strong. Though his deeds were brave and his arm was long, he hunted with the tribe, for he had learned the wisdom of the Cave Dwellers. He knew that it was not safe for a man or a woman to fight alone. The least of the forest enemies was able to destroy them. The strong men had wandered into the forest to return no more. But when the tribe went forth great deeds were possible, even the sabre-toothed tiger had been destroyed by the thrusts of many. It was the strength of all the Cave people that made safe the lives of every one.

BIG FOOT'S NEW WEAPON

The great flood that came in the spring brought death and misery to the tribes of savages that lived upon the banks of the river. Many were drowned in the swift waters, while others were borne away and scattered in strange lands. A few members of the tribe of Cave Dwellers found safety in the trees near the old Hollow. Far below, many of their brothers and sisters, with the men and women of other tribes, clung to the great trees where they also found security.

Strong Arm, Quack Quack, and little Laughing Boy were among these. With the Foolish One and the Hairy Man they lived in the great banyan until the river crept back into its old channel. Then they descended upon the earth once more and began their long journey toward the Hollow, where they had lived with a small group of Cave Dwellers, the people of their own tribe.

All the face of the world seemed covered with a layer of rich mud, deposited by the river. The sun grew warmer with every day and a hot steam arose continually from the earth. Strong Arm and his little band made their way slowly, for the moist air gave them a fever and weakened them. Always it was very difficult to find food, for the roots lay buried in the soft mud. It was necessary to search in the branches of the trees for the nests of birds, and occasionally they found a few gulls' eggs.

For two nights they had slept in the limbs of trees, while Strong Arm watched wearily lest an enemy approach.

Already at this early stage in their journey the rank grasses of the tropics were springing up. A thousand creeping things thrust out their heads from the mud and slime. And the tracks of the black bear, the

International Socialist Review 10 (October 1909): 327–32.

wooly-haired rhinoceros and the sabre-toothed tiger were seen once more along the river bank.

Very cautiously this small band of savages advanced, for they had only rough sticks to use in defending themselves. On the third day they had traveled but a little way and of eggs they found none, nor any other thing. Their stomachs cried for food and they ventured beyond the skirts of the wood, where dangers lurked, seeking something with which to satisfy their hunger.

Strong Arm advanced, with caution, ahead of the little party. When he had gone but a little way, before him, from the cane, there arose suddenly a huge man. He was taller than any man among the tribe of the Cave Dwellers, and with a stout stick he struck Strong Arm a blow on the head that dashed him to the ground. Though the arm of the big man was swift, it was not much quicker than Quack Quack, who threw herself upon him from behind. Laughing Boy added his blows to hers, scratching and biting the legs of the stranger with all his young power, till he also lay motionless.

A soft movement in the cane announced the presence of another and more wary enemy. But the blows of Quack Quack, the Hairy Man, and the Foolish One soon drove him from cover, where they beat him freely, till he threw up his hands in a gesture of submission.

Then, borne on the winds that swept the old forest, came a faint smell of fresh meat to the nostrils of the hungry group. The anger of the travelers was soon forgotten and Strong Arm now commanded the two strangers to lead them to the feast. With a great show of friendliness, they limped forward and conducted their victors to a fire that blazed above a pile of rocks.

And they poked away the coals that covered a basin fashioned among the stones, like a great oven. Covered with large leaves, lay the roasted body of a man, which the two strangers dragged steaming from the flames. Then the Cave Dwellers and the strangers seized each his portion of the meat and fell to eating. And the flesh of the roasted man seemed very good to them.

Till the new moon grew round and full, the Cave People and the Hairy Man remained with the strangers, while the water slowly drained off the swampy river banks and the way toward their old home in the Hollow became more safe.

They now had always the wonderful Fire with which to protect themselves against the forest animals. No caves there were and the trees abounded with the green snakes and many other enemies, but for all these the small group of men and Quack Quack, the woman, were not harmed.

Upon the rocks they kept the fire burning continually and at night they slept securely while some among them fed the blaze.

Very soon the Cave People began to call the shorter of the two strangers Big Foot, because his feet were very long. The other they called Tall, on account of his extreme height.

Although Strong Arm, Quack Quack, and the Foolish One were from tribes strange to Big Foot and Tall, they were all able to understand each other perfectly, by means of the simple gesture language common to all tribes in the lower stage of savagery. Thus, the Hairy Man, from still another tribe, had no difficulty in making himself understood, nor in learning the thoughts or wishes of his companions.

One day, when hunting, the little band came upon a flint pit. To the Cave People the old gravel bed meant nothing, but Tall and Big Foot became greatly excited, and they grabbed the flakes that had become chipped from the flint cores and dashed them violently against a great stone lying near. Faint sparks flew. Then Tall covered the rocks with the feathers of a dead fowl and struck among them with the flint flake. Soon the feathers were ignited by the sparks. And Strong Arm and Quack Quack marveled at the Fire Beast which the strange rock had been able to summon.

The tribe from whence Tall and Big Foot came, had long known the use of flint in kindling fires, and well they knew the treasures they had found. From them the Cave People learned, also, and Strong Arm and Quack Quack bore with them always thereafter, one of these strange and wonderful stones, with which they soon became able to call forth the Fire Beast to their protection.

More and more, as the days passed, Tall taught them wonderful things. The flesh they cooked remained sweet for many days and did not grow rank with time, as raw meat did. Thus a new hope sprang up in the hearts of the Cave People, for armed with these rude flints, they were able at any time to kindle a fire and protect themselves from the forest enemies. Also they cooked their food, and this made possible the long, dangerous journey to the land of their fathers.

In spite of the height of Tall and the long limbs and great muscles of Big Foot, they wished always to carry out the desires of Quack Quack. Not only was she a woman, and for all women they cherished a great tenderness, but also was she strong, and both these men were unable to forget the blows she had given them when first they had attacked the Cave Dwellers and their little band. To Quack Quack, therefore, they looked for commands and they obeyed her words and gestures, while they sought her good will. But in spite of all this, Strong Arm remained the leader over all, for he was able to stand up before any man in the group, and the words which he spoke and the desires he made known were always for the good of the band.

So it came about naturally that when Strong Arm and Quack Quack signified their desire to return to the Hollow, which was the old home of the Cave People, that the Hairy Man, Tall, and Big Foot gave heed to them.

And they all made preparations for the journey. The large bones which they had found, were made formidable, when they were cracked and split open at end. Also they gathered knotted limbs from the trees, which the Cave People were accustomed to wave savagely around their heads, crushing in the skulls of the enemy.

But they prized nothing so highly as the rough pieces of flint flakes which they dug from the old gravel bed. Wonder and awe they felt for these strange stones, and not a little fear. To them even inanimate things possessed life, and the small flakes of flint were only a new, queer sort of animal that had hitherto befriended them by calling forth the great Fire Beast. These might also be capable of doing them harm and it was with deep feelings of uncertainty that they first began to use these wonderful flint rocks.

In the hunt which preceded their departure, the little band were fortunate in snaring a fat young boar. They speedily killed him and dragged his body to the top of a small rocky hill. And they pulled out the loose stones, building a deep, basin-like oven into which they put the body. This they covered with green palm leaves. Then a fire was kindled over this great oven and everybody made ready for the feast.

But the fragrant odor of roast meat reached the nose of the sabre-toothed tiger and he followed the scent till he came to the small camp. And all the stray members of the little band crouched low on the opposite side of the big blaze in mortal terror. For here there were no caves in which they could take refuge and their numbers were too few for them to fight the enemy safely in the open.

But all the loose stones they had dislodged and pulled out when building the great oven, lay about them. And they gathered them up and piled them high like a great wall, for they feared an attack from the rear. And the rude wall of stones rose almost to their waists.

Very warily the tiger crept up the hill and approached the flames. The wind bore the smell of the roasting meat squarely into his teeth, and lured him on. But the wind carried, too, the thick smoke upon him, and he choked and paused to reconnoiter. As the wind died down he advanced hungrily, but the smoke and sparks from the flames sent him back to the foot of the hill.

The little band of savages watched him, while their limbs trembled and their hair stood on end. Between them and the tiger roared the tall sheet of flames, but soon he began to circle the hill seeking an easy way of attack. Below the rude wall, erected by them, the terrifying smoke and flying sparks no longer threatened. And he sniffed the air and advanced cautiously.

In the meantime, the small band of savages were rendered almost beside themselves with fear. Of weapons they had none. All their new sharp bone spears lay at the foot of the hill, with the great knotted clubs. The Foolish One started one of the big stones rolling down upon the tiger, but it passed instead of deterring him.

Then Strong Arm seized a large burning bough and hurled it straight into the great beast's face. But the tiger crouched low on the ground and the blazing torch passed over his head without harming him. Low he lay, with his long striped tail swaying to and fro, like the tail of a great cat. His eyes glowed with rage and fear and his lips were curled back in a snarl of fury.

Of all things in the old forest the strange, red, flaming fire alone had caused him to hesitate. The fierce unknown spat out a breath of hot smoke that bit into his muscular throat and choked him and the hot blaze held a menace that thrilled his long, lank body with a new fear.

Still he did not give up. Never in all his strong, free life in the forest had he ever given up. But he retreated to the foot of the hill, circling round and round it once more.

Long he continued, with his body crouched low, and his head thrown up, scenting at once the rich odor of the roasting boar, and the thick smoke, so full of strange menace.

Again and again he advanced, driven by the hunger within him, only to retreat because of the fear that would not be subdued. But as the sun sank low in the west, the little band scattered the flames and dragged out the roasted body of the young boar. From this they tore, eagerly, great chunks of the warm and dripping flesh and devoured them and one and all they thought no meat had ever tasted so sweet before.

During the feast they watched the tiger always, and they laid new branches upon the fire to keep it alive. But ere any one was filled—as savages were used to fill their stomachs after a long period of fasting—Strong Arm made known his wishes. Soon everybody understood his desire to reserve a portion of the young boar, that, should they prove unequal to the task of driving off the tiger, they might fling to him and escape.

To his wise suggestion all listened and obeyed except Big Foot, who declined to relinquish his portion. It was only after Strong Arm had thrust him down the side of the hill, threatening to hurl him to the hungry beast below, that Big Foot yielded. Once more Strong Arm had proven himself the leader of the band. Once more had his words resulted in the welfare of the group.

For, the flames having subsided a little, the smell of the meat drew old sabre-tooth irresistibly, and he made a bold and sudden dash upon the band.

But Strong Arm was quick also and a yell of warning he gave, as he threw a blazing bough upon him. But the tiger leaped over it and made his way nearer. Now the others seized burning branches and hurled them, until he must step straight upon the glowing coals to advance. And the fierce fires under his feet and the sparks and flames about him, sent the old fear through his blood and the tiger down the hill and through the forest snarling and howling with pain. Long they heard his roarings re-echoing through the old woods, but when darkness came on they descended and gathered more branches and leaves to continue the fire throughout the night.

THE FIRST PRIEST

Although Strong Arm, who was the wisest and strongest and swiftest man among the Cave People, had been dead, and in part eaten and in part buried beneath a great pile of earth and stones, the Cave People felt sure that he had not remained dead.

More than one of the members of the tribe had seen him fighting and hunting, eating and dancing, during the dreams that come in the night, and so they believed that a part of Strong Arm, the spirit or ghost part of Strong Arm, still lived. Again and again he had appeared to them in the spirit, or in dreams, to advise them about the things the tribe intended to do.

The Cave People were unable to understand these things and there was nobody to tell them that dreams were not of the world of reality. And so they believed that Strong Arm still lived, and that other dead men and women and children of the tribe still lived in the Spirit World. It was true that the spirits of these dead did not appear in the broad light of day, but the Cave People believed that they haunted their old grounds, invisible to the eyes of their tribesmen.

They believed that the spirits of the dead may return to befriend the members of the tribe, or to hinder their enemies, provided, always, that the members of the tribe enlisted their aid and their affections.

Now Big Foot, since there was no longer the wise voice of Strong Arm, nor the mighty strength of the old chief to enforce the good of his people, set himself to become the leader of the Cave People. He slashed his hairy thighs with his flint knife to prove how brave he was, allowing the gashes to become sores in order to prolong the evidence of his courage. He strutted about and waved his poison-tipped arrows when the young men refused to listen to his words. Also he rubbed the noses of all the women of the tribe and sought to caress them, attempting to

International Socialist Review 16 (June 1916): 738–741.

drive the men of the tribe from the new nests, or caves or huts, which they had built in the far North country so many moon journeys from the old hollow where little Laughing Boy was born.

Big Foot boasted with a loud voice and bullied the children and spoke soft words to the women, while he glared at the young men and urged them into the forest to hunt for food. Always he kept his poisoned darts at his side and he managed to secure for himself the tenderest portion of the young goats which the people had discovered leaping and running wild amid the sharp slopes and crags of the mountains.

So the tribe grew weary of his sorry ruling and there was much fighting and discord, which laid them open to the attacks of their many enemies.

Without doubt Big Foot was possessed of much cunning, for while other men of the tribe were as strong of limb and as fleet of foot, Big Foot was more powerful than they. Longer was his arm because he had learned first how to make and to wield his great bow and arrows almost as well as young One Ear, who had escaped from the Arrow Throwers and returned to his own people, the Cave Dwellers, bringing knowledge of the weapons of these strange enemies.

The Cave Dwellers had paused in their journeyings and battlings northward, on the banks of the lake that shone like white fire when the sun beat down upon its rolling surface. The way was new to them and unknown dangers threatened everywhere and they had utmost need to walk warily, less a new tribe descend upon them with some new weapon of destruction and turn them back into the dangers they had out-stripped.

Instead of holding the people together with wise words and instead of preparing to search out the lands to prepare for the strange evils that lie in wait for primitive man whenever he travels beyond the ways of his experience, Big Foot caused nothing but conflict. It was only his superior skill in the use of the flint-tipped arrows, which the Cave People were acquiring very rapidly, that prevented him from being slain by the members of the tribe.

Then it was that One Ear dreamed a dream. He thought that his spirit had journeyed far into the spirit world where it encountered the spirit of Strong Arm. And Strong Arm had spoken with One Ear, sending words of wisdom to the people of the tribe. He had called Big Foot the enemy of the Cave People. And when he wakened in the morning, One Ear remembered his dream. So he gathered all the people together and told them these things. And no man or woman among them knew that he spoke only of a dream. They believed that the spirit of Strong Arm still lived and that the things in One Ear's dream had actually occurred.

So the Cave People chattered together and gesticulated and stole the fresh meat Big Foot had hidden in his cave and menaced him from cover by shaking their clubs and growling like angry dogs. Big Foot fled to his branch hut, where he glared at the members of the tribe and waved his long arrows.

The Cave People had long respected the words of Strong Arm and when they heard what he had spoken to One Ear in a dream, they hated Big Foot more fiercely than ever.

At last Big Foot returned to the people of the tribe, many of whom were sitting about a wood fire, and he spoke to them, trying to gain their good will and attempting to show them that none was so swift, so strong or so brave as he. But the people screamed "Strong Arm! Strong Arm!" to remind Big Foot that the old chief had spoken against him.

And Big Foot grew frantic with the rage that came upon him. He seized the club of Strong Arm which had been given to Laughing Boy in order that he might derive from it some of the virtue of bravery which his father, Strong Arm, had possessed. Big Foot spat upon it and crushed it beneath a great stone, when he hurled the shattered fragments far out into the green waters of the lake.

All the Cave People shivered with fear, for they thought this was a very foolish thing. They believed that the spirits of the dead grow angry when their weapons are broken or destroyed and they felt sure that the spirit of Strong Arm would punish Big Foot for the desecration he had worked on the club of the old chief.

But Big Foot was too angry to be afraid. White foam appeared upon his lips when he thought of the spirit of Strong Arm and he longed for a tangible foe, with flesh upon his bones that he might crush, with red juice in his skin that he might spill, with ears and a nose that he might bite and twist and tear. He desired an enemy into whose soft belly he might hurl one of his sharp arrows.

But there were only the Cave People beside him and the menace in their eyes and their lips, pulled back, snarling from their teeth, made him afraid. So he lifted up his voice in a frenzy of hate and scorn while he called the name of "Strong Arm! Strong Arm! Maker of lies." He called him "Fool! Coward! Weak One! Baby!" and "Snake-that-crawls!" while he made violent gestures of hatred and disgust.

The Cave People watched him fearfully. To them it did not seem the part of wisdom to mock and defy the spirit of Strong Arm, which still lived, though his body had perished. Something was bound to happen. Strong Arm had never permitted any man to speak thus of him when he was living in the flesh and they did not believe his spirit would endure insult from Big Foot. Indeed, yes, something was sure to happen.

But it was not good for the whole tribe to be punished or blamed for the foolishness of Big Foot. This they knew and they made haste to put wide distances between themselves and him, pursuing their own work or their own ends with much ostentation as far as possible removed from his presence. If the spirit of Strong Arm was hiding in the valley and had chanced to overhear the evil words of Big Foot, no flat-headed savage among the tribe wanted Strong Arm to fancy he had anything to do with these things. They washed their hands of the whole affair and departed from the immediate presence of Big Foot.

The more Big Foot raved, the oftener One Ear called upon the spirit of Strong Arm, crying:

"Brave one! Wise one! Swift of foot" and "Give us of thy counsel!" And the Cave People began talking in loud voices of the good deeds of their old chief, of his courage and strength, of his wisdom and his "Eye-that-never-slept."

While Big Foot defied the spirit of Strong Arm, One Ear and the Cave People sought to propitiate him with loud words of admiration and some flattery.

"Stronger than the hairy mastodon" they called him and "Father of all the lions." He could outleap the mountain goat and outclimb the longest armed ou-rang-oo-tang. His voice was like the thunder and his breath like the winds that bend the trees on the river banks.

They felt more certain than ever that something was going to happen. They expected the spirit of Strong Arm to make it happen. But they did not desire to share in untoward events if a little information given to the spirit of Strong Arm could prevent this thing.

But the day passed, and the sun slid down the wings of the sky into the red fire of the lake, and still Big Foot strutted about with loud and boasting words. Still the Cave People waited and hoped, and were afraid.

And that night the spirit of Strong Arm again appeared to One Ear in a dream and his voice was fierce with anger against Big Foot and, in the dream, he counselled One Ear to tell the Cave People to push Big Foot from the tallest crag along the mountain gorge so that his body would be crushed upon the sharp stones below.

In the morning One Ear told these things to the people of the tribe and they drank the words of Strong Arm eagerly, begging Big Foot to join in a hunt for the wild goat amid the slopes of the mountain. But Big Foot was afraid and hid in his hut, making queer mouthings and snatching food from the children and waving his sharp arrows.

So the Cave People gathered about One Ear urging him to meet the spirit of Strong Arm once more and to ask for more wisdom on how to dispatch the evil man who brought dangers and conflict to the tribe.

Again in the morning One Ear called the people together, saying that the spirit of Strong Arm counselled the people to build fires about the hut of Big Foot in the night so that he might be destroyed.

And so, when darkness wrapped the valley in her soft folds, the Cave People stole from their shelters, each bearing branches and glowing coals from the camp fire, which they hurled in the door of Big Foot, with stones and spears so that he might not escape and injure the tribe.

The night was black and Big Foot was unable to hit the people with his sharp arrows. Coals were thrown upon the dry thatch of his hut and soon the flames encircled him with their burning tongues.

And when it was discovered that his body was burned to ashes and that the spirit of Big Foot had escaped, the Cave People rejoiced in their hearts. But their lips were dumb. For the first time they spoke well of Big Foot, whom they hated in their hearts. For was not the fate of Big Foot proof of the foolishness of speaking ill of the dead! Was not the victory of the Cave People who had spoken well of Strong Arm proof of their wisdom in these things?

The Cave People believed the spirit of Big Foot would be actively inimical to the tribe, just as they believed that the spirit of Strong Arm had proved itself to be the friendly father of the people.

And One Ear continued to dream dreams, which he related to the Cave People, giving them words of wisdom and courage from the spirit of Strong Arm and evil words from the spirit of Big Foot. Thus they grew to believe wondrous things of Strong Arm. His virtues grew with the passing of the suns, just as his strength increased and his wisdom was extolled until he became almost a god to the people of the tribe.

And when ill befell the Cave People, One Ear told them it had been caused by the evil spirit of Big Foot and when they escaped from these evils, he reported how the spirit of Strong Arm had befriended the tribe. Always was One Ear dreaming dreams. He told how the spirit of Strong Arm had counselled the people to make of Big Nose their leader and chief, which they did.

As he grew in years and in power, One Ear demanded that the best joints of meat, the warmest place by the fire, the safest cave or hut, be his portion. These things he declared were the commands of Strong Arm.

And so One Ear became a great man of the tribe. When the forest fire swept the plains and drove the wild fowl and the forest animals far inland, and brought famine to the Cave People, One Ear reported that the spirit of Strong Arm had done these things to punish the people because they had not brought young fowl, of which he was very fond, every day to One Ear.

Thus One Ear became the first priest of the tribe, protected before other men in order that the good spirits might not take vengeance upon the tribe should ill befall him. People brought him sharp knives and soft skins with which he made himself warm when the far northern winds blew cold in the winter time. And One Ear said good words to the great spirits for these bearers of gifts, so that they might be prospered and escape the sharp tooth of the crocodile.

By and by there came other dreamers of dreams who spoke with the great spirits and also brought messages to the people. Strong arms of the tribe clashed and there were great battles among the Cave People, till the Pretenders were slain, when once more peace and harmony reigned within the valley upon the shores of the great lake.

7

Rhymes and Poems

MARCY'S last book, *Rhymes of Early Jungle Folk,* a collection of short verses intended to acquaint children with an outline of prehistory, was published just before her death. Praised in the IWW weekly *Industrial Solidarity* as "a book that levelheaded parents with an eye to beauty and with respect for the intelligence of their children will stuff into the Christmas stockings of all sizes from five years old to fifteen and even fifty,"[1] it includes fifty-four rhymes, many of them closely related to her earlier "Stories of the Cave People." The rhymes reprinted here are typical of the humor and sparkling language that characterize the entire collection.

With the exception of the brief verses printed on the "Socialist Playing Cards" offered for sale by Charles H. Kerr & Company beginning in 1911, the selections that follow the verses reprinted from *Rhymes of Early Jungle Folk* are the only other poems by Marcy to have been published. Following her death, a group of Mary's friends planned to put together a book of the poems she had recited to them over the years, but the project never materialized.

Note

1. *Industrial Solidarity,* 16 December 1922.

Rhymes of Early Jungle Folk

CHANGE! CHANGE! CHANGE!

The change was abrupt,
But it did interrupt
    The lazy reptilian rule;
Perhaps the earth tipped,
And its axis was slipped
    To the poles we have heard of in school.

The weather turned cold,
And the Winter grew bold;
    He reigned over most of the year,
While the reptiles, with skin
Which was naked and thin,
    Succumbed in a bleak atmosphere.

But the few that had fur,
As it chanced to occur,
    Were all dressed to exist in the snow;
The hairy and feathered,
Adapted, so weathered
    The winds, and the ice and the blow!

The Age Ce-no-zo-ic
Required the stoic,
    In order to grow and survive,
A living contraption,
With gifts of adaption,
    And the mammals began to arrive.

The beech and the hollys,
Say the wise anthropollys,
    Appeared with the ivy and gum,
And trees of new classes,
And plains with their grasses,
    And flowers where honey bees hum.

It was during this time,
That a drama sublime
    Made the earth's surface crumple and shrink,
And the mountains arose;
As geology shows,
    There were portions beginning to sink.

With a giant upheaving,
Himalyas were cleaving
    The air and the clouds and the sky,

The Alps and the Andes,
A pair of high grandees,
   Who smile on the life passing by!

And soon there were birds with their feathered protection,
   Who watched over eggs in a nest,
     Till, birdies arriving,
     They fed them, contriving
   To teach them the ways that were best.

These warm-blooded creatures were very much wiser
   Than the former reptilian crew,
     With instinctive affection,
     Maternal protection,
   Instructed their little ones new.

And Oh! they were busy, for hunting and mating
   Meant ventures they never had known;
     And so through their fearings,
     Their bearing and rearings,
   Developed a brain of their own.

For brains are developed by seeing and doing,
   By living, and caring, and strife;
     They grow with our muscles,
     Through ventures and tussles,
   And all that we live in a life!

They do not fall down like the rains from the heavens,
   Which water the fields and the grains,
     'Tis just by diffusing,
     By living and using,
   That creatures grow wonderful brains!

THE EARLY PITH-E-CAN-THRO-PUS

Before the time of cave men,
   In the early Pli-o-cene,
There lived a pack of wild things,
   All hairy, squat and lean;

They fought with tooth and sharp nails,
   And wielded mighty stones;
That they walked as you and I do,
   Is proven by their bones.

They had no tools or weapons;
   They feared the fire too;
They hid and skulked, and shivered,
   As weaker creatures do.

They did not have a language;
    Could scarcely speak at all,
But grunted sounds of portent,
    Should good or ill befall.

They heard the tiger roar, when
    He gorged upon his kill,
And when he had departed,
    Crept out to eat their fill.

In wood, or swamp, or jungle,
    Or out upon the plains,
They hurried forth in numbers,
    And stole the grim remains.

And when they met a stranger,
    They hit him on the head,
And ate, and ate, these cannibals,
    Till all the pack was fed.

* * *

Perhaps a million years ago,
    The human race began,
For the early pith-e-can-thro-pus
    E-rect-us was a MAN!

O WHAT WOULD WE DO WITHOUT THUMBS?

Thumbs! Thumbs!
O what could we do without thumbs?
    We couldn't do baking,
    Nor building, nor raking,
We couldn't play fiddles or drums!

Dear! Dear!
We would be very awkward, I fear!
    We couldn't do sowing,
    Nor digging, nor rowing;
O wouldn't the people seem queer!

My! My!
And how could we eat apple pie?
    Or wipe off our noses,
    Or button our clotheses?
We would be like the dogs—you and I!

For—For—
We could not even open a door,
    Nor play ball for pleasure,
    Nor weigh things, nor measure—
Why—we wouldn't be FOLKS any more!

Drums! Drums!
The key to a mystery comes!
    The Cave Folks could beat them,
    The foes that would eat them—
Because they had fingers and thumbs!

THE FIRST PRIEST

    The chief of the Cave Folks,
        Was tall Strong Arm,
    The first on the trail,
        Or to give an alarm;
    The longest, the strongest,
        He taught them to know
    The paths which were safe,
        And the ways they should go.

    But now he was crushed
        By a pain-maddened bear,
    Protecting her cubs
        Hid away in her lair.
    They buried him deep,
        And they covered his bed,
    With earth and with stones
        And they placed at his head,
    Pink tubers, and fishes,
        And baskets of meat,
    That he might not lack food
        When his spirit would eat.

    They knew that his spirit
        Was hovering near,
    And they made a lament
        To his mythical ear:
    "Oh! Spirit," they cried,
        "Pray you tell us the way
    "To find a new chief,
        "Lest we wander astray."

    And as the nights passed,
        And the people awoke,
    The Lazy One
        Fooled all these credulous folk.
    "The spirit of Strong Arm
        "Remembers our plight,
    "And brings me commands,
        "As I sleep in the night;
    "He bids you choose Oof
        "As your chief and your guide,

"And commands me give counsel,
  "For Him, at his side."
And the Cave Folks believed
  In this primitive priest,
And gave him the tenderest meat,
  At the feast.

PUZZLES AND THINGS

He stared at his reflection in the water,
And gathered stones to drive the youth away;
He brandished spear, for he was ripe for slaughter,
But his water image mocked him from the bay;
He couldn't understand it, for the thing was always there,
And when he dived he could not find the fellow any where;
So down he sat upon the bank,
And give him stare for stare.

And when he walked, this Neolithic youngster,
He saw his shadow pacing with his stride,
And ran a dozen metres to evade him,
But the silent fellow galloped at his side;
He could not understand it, and he racked his feeble mind,
The shadow seemed to run as fast as any startled hind,
And so he glowered at the shade
He could not leave behind.

And when he found a spring among the caverns,
And whooped his joy, an eerie play began;
The walls caught up his song of happy triumph,
And echoes sent it flying back again,
Repeated every song he sung, and mimicked every call;
He could not understand the voices in the cavern wall,
And hunted for a human trail,
Which was not there at all.

And when he fell asleep upon his bear skin,
He often dreamed and thought his dreams were true;
He killed a giant mammoth with his arrow,
And forests full of hairy people slew;

But when he waked and bragged about his valor, strong and deep,
The folks who tend the fire, and the silent watches keep,
Shook their heads in grave denial:
"You were in the cave asleep!"
He sometimes saw the dead chief in his dreaming,
And heard his voice commanding all the men;
He thought the dead were only dead in seeming;
And fall asleep to one day hunt again;

He gazed at his reflection, and his shadow, and he thought:
The world is filled with spirit folks, and puzzles spirit-wrought;
It is wisdom to respect them, and
I had as lief as not.

IF EVERYTHING GREW UP

If every little cherry stone
    Became a cherry tree,
And every egg the fishes laid
    Grew up to swim to sea,
        The world would be a funny place;
        I fear it could not find the space,
        For you and me and cousin Grace
    To live contentedly.

The cherry trees would fill the streets,
    And where the houses band,
And farms and woods. The cherry trees
    Would cover all the land!
        The sea would be a seething mass
        Of fish where steaming vessels pass,
        And you and I—Alack! Alas!
    Would have no place to stand!

The more I think, the more I know,
    I hate to see things die;
And though I cannot eat enough
    Of mother's cherry pie,
        Perhaps we'd better not complain,
        While things in status quo remain,
        But take the joys that we may gain,
    As every day runs by.

Rhymes of Early Jungle Folk (Chicago: Charles H. Kerr & Co., 1922), 22–25, 29, 70–71, 84–85, 100–102, 112.

If Socialism Came

There was a man in Blanktown,
    Of kind and foolish bent,
Who loved to tell his neighbors
    What Socialism meant.

On every summer evening
    He'd haunt the market square,
And loud, in fiery tirade,
    His voice would rend the air.

He whaled the corporations,
    He flayed the "soulless Trust";
His jaw worked fast and faster
    As he pawed the air and cussed;
He said old Rockefeller
    Was a "human fiend," and then
He spat upon the sidewalk,
    And called him names again.

He "stood for lower taxes,"
    And thundered with a wail.
That the "new administration
    Ought to build a stronger jail"!
He sought dramatic climax,
    Acquired rural fame,
In telling how they'd run things
    "When Socialism came"!

This foolish man in Blanktown,
    His words would scorch and burn,
Was so busy teaching Blanktown,
    He hadn't time to LEARN!—
This crazy man in Blanktown,
    (And so he went to seed)
With his everlasting talking,
    He had no time to READ!

It was talking in the evening,
    And talking through the day,
He slew the Rich Man with his tongue,
    And talked his life away.
And if you go to Blanktown,
    You'll find him in the square,
Still railing at the Council,
    And the "Deals that are not square"!

"Free text-books" are his hobby,
    And he'll keep you on the jump,
Over "Prohibition" futures,
    And a new town pump!
This foolish man in Blanktown,
    He chatters just the same,
On "how they'd clean the streets, sir,
    If Socialism came"!

All his talk about "low taxes,"
    What's that to do with ME?
I do not care a rap about
    How clean "the streets would be;"
Such pictures of "the Future,"
    Seem to me a trifle THIN,
And the Deal that interests ME,
    Is where do I COME IN!

And I think this man at Blanktown's
    A simple-minded fool,
Whose head is filled with sawdust
    From the Populistic School.
And if his dope to Blanktown,
    In Socialism's name,
Is right, I'd go to Boston,
    When Socialism came.

In Josephine R. Cole and Grace Silver, comps., *Socialist Dialogues and Recitations* (Chicago: Charles H. Kerr & Co., 1913), 55–56.

The Fate of the College Graduate

There was a College Graduate; he had a Noble Brow;
    We thought that he knew everything, was IT,
        IT, IT.
We thought that if he hadn't come to teach the workers
        HOW,
    We should never have progressed a little bit, bit,
        bit.

He volunteered to lead us, and we handed him the job,
    He wanted so to help the world along, long, long,
And he wrote a little booklet, and sold it to the Mob;
    And showed us that the Plutocrats were wrong,
        wrong, wrong.

One day he went a-walking in an absent-minded way,
    A-thinking of a Book he had in view, view, view.
At a lonely railroad crossing 'twas a passing freight,
        they say.
    Cut his massive Cerebellum right in two, two, two.

I thought the sun would darken, and daylight turn to
        night,
    And I didn't look for Pay Day any more, more,
        more.
But we found we didn't need him to sit and boss the
        fight.

And my wages are nine-fifty as before, fore,
    fore.

The wheels kept on revolving, and the factory whistle
    blew,
    And our stomachs forced us ever to the game, game,
        game.
The sun is really shining, and it's quite a comfort, too,
    With the Struggle going forward just the same, same,
        same.

In Josephine R. Cole and Grace Silver, comps., *Socialist Dialogues and Recitations* (Chicago: Charles H. Kerr & Co., 1913), 57.

It's Up to You!

I do not heed the Preacher when he tells us to forbear,
And I don't like wild effusions over "deals that SHOULD BE SQUARE,"
But when I hear a Socialist bewail his sordid lot,
Berating all the Upper Dogs, I say it makes me HOT!

    For it's up to me and you, Boys!
        It's up to US today.
    You'll never see the man on top
        Abbreviate his stay.
    So do a little work, Boys,
        Annex our brothers, too,
    And bear the thought in mind, that
        It's up to me and you!

There is no use in fuming o'er the capitalist's lot;
He simply has the things today we WANT and HAVEN'T got;
He's keen about his interests, and he takes the way to WIN,
And it's folly yelling, "Robber! Renegade!" or "Crime" and "Sin!"

    'Cause it's simply up to you, Boys!
        Old Rockefeller's wise,
    We'll get his abdication
        When we're angels in the skies;
    So pull yourselves together,
        And what'er you think or do,
    Remember this is OUR fight;
        It's up to me and YOU!

You can't persuade the cat, Boys, to let the bird go free;
He doesn't care a rap about what conduct "OUGHT" to be;
He doesn't care a rap while we go OUR SEPARATE ways;
While we are not UNITED, it's the MILLIONAIRE who STAYS!

So give yourselves a hunch, Boys,
   The Upper Ten are ON;
They'll be living in their luxury
   When we are dead and gone,
If we do not get together,
   Do not cease to wait and stew!
And recognize the fact—that
   It's up to me and you!

Just spend a little; get our fellow workmen to unite!
A word from Marx will show how proletarians can fight;
And put your shoulders to the wheel, for that's the only way,
And push the fight until the Under Dog shall have his Day!

For it's up to me and you, Boys!
   The Other Fellow's wise,
He's like a sleepy cat until
   We start to ORGANIZE;
And you cannot blame the cat, Boys,
   For what YOU LET HIM DO;
So it's simply up to us, Boys,
   It's up to me and you!

In Josephine R. Cole and Grace Silver, comps., *Socialist Dialogues and Recitations* (Chicago: Charles H. Kerr & Co., 1913), 58–59.

My God

An hundred peoples
Have fashioned their gods,
And I shall fashion mine.

He shall be a god of thunder,
Of fire and of storm,
And he shall sweep away old worlds,
For me and the foundlings,

He shall build a new world,
And, with the foundlings,
I shall sit upon the topmost mountain,
And laugh through my tears;
And see the Kings of Today
Kneel at the feet of Tomorrow.

In Jack Carney, *Mary Marcy* (Chicago: Charles H. Kerr & Co., 1922), 13.

Song of the Swamp

Only a little and she comes;
Only a little waiting.
She is my spider lily with golden feet,
With golden feet that lie in the hollow of my hand;
Red are her lips as the u-pon berries,
And the savor of her is young and sweet;
Sweeter than jasamine and the wild honeysuckle
Is the savor of her.

Only a little and she comes;
I am waiting for her in the swamp;
I am waiting for her beneath the live oak,
where waited my fathers an hundred years ago.
My song is hushed;
I shall wait quietly for my love;
But my heart is the mullet
Leaping from the waters of the river in spring;
My love for her is the arms of all the pear trees
In blossom, flinging themselves upward.
She is the straight pine, pungent and clean;
I am the fingers of the Wind,
Waiting in the swamp.

The moon has reached the top of the cedar tree;
Yet a little waiting and the first song of the whip-poor-will
Will tell me she is coming,
My wild canary.
Then I shall see her swaying in the cane brake;
I shall see her cross the pontoon;
She will come swiftly,
For she knows I am waiting for her,
Waiting in the swamp.

Shadows are growing heavy with the night;
The waves of the river are kissing the feet of the lillies,
As I shall kiss the feet of my spider lily.
Ah! The first song;
The cane bends low as she comes,
My shy canary!

Soon we shall dance upon the white sands!
We shall bathe in the purple pools,
And the movement of her limbs
Will leave shadows of gold
Where she touches the waters;

Phosphorescent, she will leave
Showers of gold and silver as she passes.
And in the swamp,
I shall croon to her all the night.

In Jack Carney, *Mary Marcy* (Chicago: Charles H. Kerr & Co., 1922), 14.

8

Why Women Are Conservative

THE 1910s was a decade marked by considerable feminist activity and agitation. While the number of women taking part in feminist organizations was small, their impact was significant and they anticipated many of the causes and themes of the feminists of the 1970s and 1980s, including the need of women for personal development and self-realization. Convinced that most roles in society were culturally, rather than biologically determined, the feminists of the 1910s wanted male and female children to be raised according to human, not sexual, values and they looked forward to an open society in which the individual could develop his or her potential without regard to gender. Many feminists advocated sexual freedom and marched for the free distribution of information on birth control—activities considered shockingly radical in an era when sex was not a topic discussed openly in public.

A sizable number of these feminists were Socialists, and their presence within the party provoked sharp debate over the question of woman's emancipation. Some party members, women as well as men, believed that "the woman question" was a secondary issue. They argued that the situation of women should not be treated as a problem separate from the goal of emancipating the masses as a whole, that concern for women as a special group would divert attention from the primary revolutionary struggle. Socialist feminists, on the other hand, maintained that the economic and political oppression to which women were subjected was unique and warranted a special campaign within the class struggle. Doubly enslaved by the burdens of class and sex, women—especially working women—needed to be doubly emancipated.

Mary Marcy was among those Socialists who believed that "the woman question" was a secondary issue, that it was the class struggle that was paramount. While she in no sense regarded women as the inferior sex (on the contrary, she considered women "intellectually capable of all that men can do"), she shared August Bebel's conviction, expressed decades earlier in *Woman under Socialism*, that "The complete emancipation of woman and her equality with man . . . is possible only by a social change that shall abolish the rule of man over man—hence also of capitalism over workingmen."[1] The proper question for Socialist comrades, Marcy affirmed in the *New York Call* of 8 May 1910, "is not 'What shall the MEN do?' or 'What shall the WOMEN do?' but 'What shall WE do?' "[2] She praised Lena Morrow Lewis, the first woman to be elected to the party's national executive committee, for opposing women's organizational autonomy and stressing the primacy of the class struggle over women's emancipation.

That Marcy antagonized many feminists was less the result of her insistence that "the woman question" was a secondary issue than of her critical treatment of such presumed feminist causes as "free love." Feminists found particularly offensive her 1921 play *A Free Union: A One Act Comedy of "Free Love."* It relates how James Humboldt, an impecunious painter, is maltreated by Sonia Barowski, a "free woman" with whom he shares an apartment in Chicago. When James rebels and announces his intention to marry his long-neglected fiancée, Jean Ward, Sonia, enraged, tells him that he "belongs" to her and that she will not give him up. As he prepares to move out of the apartment, James complains of Sonia's brand of "freedom" to Jean: "You see how deep her philosophy of Freedom goes. It applies to her, but not to me or anybody else. . . . I have always been the slave. Every night her friends come up here and stay till two or three and even four o'clock in the morning, drinking and eating, lovemaking and talking about re-building the world on a nobler, more poetic plan, their plan."[3]

Excerpts from another of Marcy's writings that drew fire from feminists, *Women as Sex Vendors, or Why Women are Conservative*, constitute the selection that appears below. Coauthored by her brother Roscoe B. Tobias (who contracted terminal cancer and committed suicide during the early 1930s), it was praised highly by the noted editor and satirist H. L. Mencken, and a Japanese version of it was in press at the time of Mary's death. Her friend Jack Carney claims in his memorial pamphlet *Mary Marcy* that *Women as Sex Vendors* was written to expose "the alleged scientific pretensions of those who claimed to know and understand the sex question."[4] Fred Thompson, a long-time member of the IWW who authored the official history of the union published in 1955, offers a more extended view of the work's intent. In a letter written to this editor on 23 June 1976, Thompson comments:

> I judge Mary Marcy's purpose . . . was by irony, and by taking a tongue-in-cheek Devil's Advocate role, to get both Menckenites and his "booboisie," to start paying some heed to some unheeded consequences of our commodity culture, especially as it influenced sex roles. She was surely fully aware that her Devil's Advocate case hinged on ignoring the balancing aspect of the male role among wage slaves. It was one more means of projecting her continuing tocsin "LIVES Are

Being Sold." At that time, 1918, I recall Socialists telling me that readying people in the U.S. and Britain for woman suffrage was a device to add their conservative votes to offset growing male radicalism. The question in the title did warrant serious consideration, and she was trying to secure consideration for it in her own impish way.

Notes

1. August Bebel, *Woman Under Socialism* (New York: New York Labor News, 1904), 113. The work was originally published in Zurich in 1879.
2. "Efficiency the Test," *New York Call*, 8 May 1910.
3. Mary E. Marcy, *A Free Union: A One Act Comedy of "Free Love"* (Chicago: Charles H. Kerr & Co., 1921), 46.
4. Jack Carney, *Mary Marcy* (Chicago: Charles H. Kerr & Co., 1922), 7.

Excerpts from
Women as Sex Vendors, or Why Women Are Conservative

We have often heard discussions of the reason we do not find women, as a sex, in the vanguard of world affairs, why the great educators, strong figures in progressive or revolutionary movements, are men rather than women; why these movements, themselves, are made up almost entirely of men rather than women. People have asked over and over again why, in the fields of the arts, the sciences, in the world of "practical affairs," men, rather than women, generally excel.

We believe the answer lies in the fact that women, as a sex, are the owners of a commodity vitally necessary to the health and well-being of man. Women occupy a more fortunate biologic, and in many countries, a more fortunate economic position, in the increasingly intensified struggle for existence. And the preferred class, the biologically and economically favored class, or sex, has rarely been efficient-to-do, has never been revolutionary to attack a social system that accords advantage to it.

As a sex, women have rarely been rebels or revolutionists. We do not see how they can ever be as long as there exists any system of exploitaton to revolt against. Revolt comes from the submerged, never from the group occupying a favored place. Today the revolutionist is he who has nothing to sell but his labor power. . . .

As a sex, women . . . possess a commodity to sell or to barter. Men, as a sex, are buyers of, or barterers for, this commodity. The general attitude on this question of sex may be, and in fact usually is, wholly unconscious; but the fact remains that men and women meet each other, in the capitalist system, as buyers and sellers of, or barterers for, a commodity.

Scarcely anybody recognizes this fact, and those who sense it fail to understand the inevitable result upon society and upon women themselves. There is no office or saloon scrub-woman so displeasing and decrepit, no stenographer so old and so unattractive, no dish-washer so sodden, that she does not know, tucked far away in her inner consciousness, perhaps, that, if the very worst comes and she loses her job, there is the truck driver or the office clerk, the shaky-legged bar patron on the road to early locomotor ataxia, or the squint-eyed out-of-town salesman, who can be counted on to tide her over an emergency— usually for goods delivered.

When a man is out of a job and broke, he is flat on his back. His appetites, his desires cry out for satisfaction exactly as they did when he

Women as Sex Vendors, or Why Women Are Conservative (Being a View of the Economic Status of Women) (Chicago: Charles H. Kerr & Co., 1918), 9–10, 12–19, 21–29, 36–38, 49–53.

had money in his pockets to pay for the satisfaction of these appetites and these desires.

When a woman loses a job, she has always the sale of her sex to fall back upon as a last resort.

Please understand that this is in no way a criticism of the conduct of women. We desire to lay no stigma upon them. We lay no stigma upon any class or sex or group, for down at bottom, men and women do what they do because they have to do it. The more we understand the economic and biological status of any group, the more we see they are compelled to act, under the circumstances, and in the environment they occupy, precisely as they do act. In the struggle for existence today the laurels are only to those who use any and all methods to save themselves.

We only want to point out that women are able to save themselves because of their "favored" position in the biological world. Since economic interest and economic control are at the basis of all social institutions, we want to show some of the results of this sex monopoly possessed by women, and required by men.

Every group which possesses anything which is necessary to the health and well-being of any other group, is bound to be pursued, wooed, bribed, paid. The monopolistic class, or sex, in turn, learns to withhold, to barter, to become "uncertain, coy and hard to please," to enhance and raise the price of her commodity, even though the economic basis of the transaction be utterly concealed or disguised. All this is exactly as natural and inevitable as a group of wage workers demanding all they can get in payment for their labor power, or the land-owner holding up the farm renters for all the tenants will bear, or the broker selling to the highest bidder. No one is to be blamed.

The private possession of a commodity necessary to man, the lower cost of living for women, are the natural causes of lower wages for women than for men, and explains why women are actually able to live on lower wages, as a sex, than men.

Few people speak frankly about sex matters today. And still fewer understand them and their economic basis. The subject of sex is clothed in pretense. We discuss women philosophically, idealistically, sometimes from the viewpont of biology, but never from an economic and a biological standpoint, which is the only scientific basis from which to regard them.

Everywhere in the animal world except among humankind, the male possesses the gay and attractive plumage, the color and form to please the eye. Naturally he should possess them. But this is not so in the world of man. Here we find the woman decorating herself in the colorful garb. Woman has ceased to ask, "Is he beautiful?" She asks "What does he own?" or, "How much can he pay?"

Men love to dress their women in expensive clothes, to provide them with luxurious surroundings, because this advertises to the world the fact that they are able to purchase a superior, i.e., a higher priced commodity. Women give much time and spend money extravagantly in articles of conspicuous waste for the simple reason that by so doing they announce the fact that they are finer than other wonen, higher priced, of a fancier brand, possessed of better wares.

Everybody knows that the office clerk who aspires to the affections of an artistically gowned, jewel decked young woman, often spends most of his wages upon her in the hope of winning her attention. His office associates may describe her as "fancy," or speak of her as "an expensive package." And so the twenty dollar-a-week clerk magnifies his "income" in order to bribe the young lady into "giving herself" to him in exchange for his name and some sort of life-long support, provided he can produce it.

How many young wives have learned, to their chagrin, of the deceits thus practiced upon them by their husbands! Alas! The scenes that are enacted when it is discovered, after the ceremony, that the diamond engagement ring is not yet paid for, and that the mahogany furniture in the new flat so joyously selected by the young bride-elect, was bought upon the installment plan! That John earns only twenty dollars a week in the shipping room instead of the fifty a week he had declared, as assistant manager! Here the man has not paid as promised and every one feels that the woman has made a "bad bargain."

On the other hand, women disguise the economic basis of the deal in every possible way; lie, cheat, and compete in a life and death struggle with others of their sex. A thousand illusions, tricks, subtleties, hypocrisies are employed to cover the bald fact that wares are being displayed, are being bidden for by other men. The deal is smothered in chivalrous urbanities and sentimental verbiage. Unnumbered circumlocutions are resorted to to conceal the salesmanship of one who has a commodity to sell. . . .

It is generally granted that women with children are more conservative than women without children. We believe this is true only when they and their children are provided for. When a mother is left with no one to support her children, she becomes more predatory than other women in the pursuit of a new provider. Our jails and workhouses are full of unsuccessful mothers of this class, convicted of crimes against property.

Mothers are conservative when their children are secure; more predatory when they are in want. Mothers often compete successfully in making their wares attractive and in binding the male by habits and associations that hold him and induce him to continue to pay.

Among men, the possession of, and ability to support a woman in perpetuity, whom no other may touch, is honorific, a high sign of display. It announces to the world that such a man is able to hold a trophy in the struggle for existence. A monogamous wife is, in fact, an emblem of well-off-ness, and greatly to be desired.

A man does not wish to be one among a corporation of men owning a woman any more than he desires to be owner of a sixth part of an automobile. Not because there is anything more intrinsically wrong in purchasing one-sixth than six-sixths, but because, in a world where the ownership of private property is the greatest of all good things, individual ownership denotes respectability, comfort, ability to buy outright. Hence we have monogamy for wives and mistresses in general, and polygamy for men. . . .

Do not all respectable and well-meaning parents (and others not so respectable) seek gently to guide their daughters into safe matrimonial harbors where they barter themselves for a respectable meal-ticket, or an income, presumably, for life? They would be shocked beyond measure if you told them that back of all their exalted mummeries, they desired to see their daughters barter their sex for the highest and most enduring stake rather than to see them selling their labor or brain power for wages, or selling their sex on the installment, or retail plan, to the chance purchaser. Yet these are the facts.

And it is this hope of bartering their sex privileges for permanent support and the title of "wife" that keeps the girls of the working class in the same category as the small shop-keeper. Nearly every ordinary woman under ninety, hopes some day to find a man who will marry her and support her for the rest of her days. Instead of fitting herself for a trade or a profession, young women, and old women, devote their time to schemes for prevailing upon some man, to pay the ultimate price and marry them.

And so women, not every individual, but as a sex, are ever individualistic, ever competing among themselves, ever displaying their wares, ever looking for a possible purchaser of the commodity they have to sell, ever endeavoring to keep the purchaser satisfied and willing to pay more.

Human beings are human animals however much we may pretend to the contrary. In the rest of the animal world the fact of the mating season is frankly acknowledged. It has never been recognized among humankind within the period of written history. Is it possible that when women are released from economic and social coercion, this periodic mating instinct in the woman of the species may assert, or reassert, itself?

Wives and mistresses often submit to their husbands or lovers only through fear of losing economic security to the ever alert competitor. It is certain that when all men and all women have gained individual economic opportunity and security, social institutions will change also. May it not be possible that the jealousies now prevalent, because of the economic import or the social standing that the private claim on the individual brings, may vanish also? . . .

But do not imagine for a single moment that women are inferior to men. Biology has long since proven that daughters inherit the same natural tendencies from their fathers and their grandfathers, their mothers and their grandmothers that sons do. In the case of the girls it is only as it would be if the sons in a family all inherited a share in the monopoly of a commodity that half the human race requires. . . .

Women are intellectually capable of all that men can do. They always will be because the paternal branch of the family bequeathes to its daughters the same natural tendencies and capacities that are the heritage of its sons. It is biologically impossible for sons to inherit the cumulative capacities of their fathers alone just as it is biologically impossible for the daughters to inherit from their mothers alone. So that, at birth, it appears that both sexes must remain on an equal footing so far as heredity is concerned. But the social and economic environment differentiates. Boys and girls learn to differ more than they differ physically at birth.

We believe it is due to the fact that woman, biologically possessed of a necessary commodity, something to sell besides her labor power, leans and reckons upon this ownership, which prevents her, not individually, but as a sex, from taking an active and permanent part in the affairs and workshops of the world today. There are exceptions to the rule, of course. And often, unconsciously, perhaps, she seeks to excel in the fields occupied by the men who surround her, for the purpose of enhancing her wares.

It is to be remembered that in nearly all phases of the relations between men and women, both are almost always at least partially unconscious of the economic basis of the bargain they make, although, legally, marriage is a contract. Here society and social institutions protect the possible future mothers of the race.

We are in no way denying the existence of affection between the sexes. We see undoubted instances of self-sacrifice (in the economic sense) on the part of women everywhere. We are not gainsaying these. We only claim that the root of the relation of the sexes in America is today the economic basis of buyers and sellers of a commodity and that this basis of sex, sold as a commodity, affects every phase of our social life, and all of our social institutions, and that we fail to recognize these economic roots because of the leaves upon the social tree.

Why, do you imagine, the woman who brings to a penniless husband, not only herself but a fortune as well, is looked down upon in many countries? Why is the woman of the streets, who spends her sex earnings upon her lover, scorned universally? Is it not because both are, unconsciously violating the code, or the trade "understandings," in giving not only of themselves, but their substance as well? These women are selling below the market, or scabbing on the job. . . .

Women are potential parasites even if they never become real ones, and this is the gist of the matter we are discussing. Why are nearly all small farmers reactionary, individualistic, distrustful, competitive? Because they hope some day to become gentleman farmers. Why are most small business men narrow, egoistic, conservative? For the reason that they hope one day to become men of Big Business. The young woman in America today possesses the same psychology. Being young, she not only hopes, she expects, to rise into the leisure class when some young man asks her for the privilege of supporting her through life.

We are making no claim that the lot of millions of housekeeping mothers, married to workingmen, is more enviable than is the condition of their husbands. We merely wish to point out that millions of women, potentially, actually, or psychologically, are "of the leisure class," and that fact and expectation keep women, as a sex, allied to the forces of reaction. When a woman is competing in a life and death struggle among a score of other young women, to make a permanent legal bargain which entails the promise of an income or support for life, she has little leisure or energy to spare in making over, or revolutionizing the present social system.

The mind of the average woman today is that of the petty shopkeeper. Entertaining, ofttimes, impossible dreams, these dreams, are, nevertheless, productive of a conservative and bourgeois ideology of a life of leisure and non-productiveness. . . .

Of course, every one knows that marriage is a legal contract; but whom does it bond? Certainly not the woman, nor any woman in America. For she may easily free herself and even divorce and penalize her husband if she is dissatisfied either with him or his earnings; or she may evade all the obligations she is supposed to meet, almost always with absolute impunity.

Whatever she may do or leave undone in the marriage relation, if it but be with sufficient pretense and discretion, in America, at least, the world and the courts absolve her from all blame.

If she be discreet, she may entertain lovers galore; she may refuse to perform any of the theoretical duties of the home; she may refuse to bear children or to surrender to her husband, without censure, and often without the knowledge of the world. If she be addicted to drunkenness, people will divine that her husband must have treated her brutally; if she be seen with other men, folks suspect that he neglects her.

If her husband seeks satisfaction for his desires elsewhere, she may divorce him and secure alimony; if he deserts her the law will return him to her side, if it can find him. If he fails to bring home the wherewithal to provide for her, she may have him sent to jail. If she discovers that he is getting the affection and the sex life which she has denied him, outside of his home, and if she buys a revolver and murders him in cold blood, the jury will exonerate her.

If a wife deserts her husband and her children, the law does not make her a criminal; for wife abandonment, the husband is held criminally liable.

No matter what the offense of the woman, custom and public opinion demand that every "decent" man permit his wife to accuse him on "just grounds" and to secure the divorce and call on the law to force him to pay her alimony for the rest of their natural lives.

No matter what the provocation, legally or sentimentally, no man can be exonerated for killing a woman. No matter how little the provocation, legally or sentimentally, any woman may kill almost any man, and the jury will render a verdict of Not Guilty. She has only to say that he "deceived her."

A husband may become crippled or invalided and there is no law even suggesting that it is the duty of his wife to support him; most communities would lynch a man who neglected a sick or helpless wife, and the law would certainly deal most harshly with him. The law throws no safeguards about the man, to protect him against his wife's failure to live up to her theoretical marital obligations, to protect him when he is ill, or in the enjoyment of separate maintenance, alimony, or against non-support or abandonment.

The laws today protect the owners of property and the economically powerful. The more economic power a group, or a class, or a sex possesses, the more the state throws the mantle of its protective laws about it. Women are owners of a commodity for which men are buyers or barterers, and our modern laws protect woman at the expense of man. . . .

The propertyless woman today is rarely reduced to starvation. If the price (or wages) offered for the sale of her laboring power are unsatisfactory, she may always supplement them through the barter or sale of her sex. That there are no women hoboes in the civilized world today is incontestable proof of the superiority of the economic status of woman over man. . . .

9

Capitalism and War

WHEN World War I broke out in August 1914 and the great majority of socialists in each of the belligerent nations rallied to the flag, Marcy was heartsick. In believing that her comrades across the Atlantic would prevent war, or at least never support such a conflict should it come, she had sadly underestimated the strength of European nationalism. Together with other members of the Socialist Party of America she had mistakenly assumed that the power of the socialist parties and their cohesion in the Second International constituted an insurmountable obstacle to a major war. Had not the international socialist congresses held at Stuttgart in 1907 and Copenhagen in 1910 clearly affirmed the notion of working-class solidarity and adopted resolutions against war?

The national executive committee of the Socialist Party of America issued its first statement on the conflict in Europe just days after England declared war on Germany. It declared the party's "oppositon to this and all other wars, waged on any pretext whatsoever" and urged "the national administration to prove the genuineness of its policy of peace by opening immediate negotiations for mediation and extending every effort to bring about the speedy termination of this disastrous conflict."[1] In subsequent statements released over the next two years, the party warned of a food shortage and demanded that the government seize food industries in order to "starve the war and feed America"; charged that capitalism "logically leads to war"; called upon American workers to oppose war agitation; adopted a peace program using the formula "no indemnities and no annexations"; and attacked both the "jingoistic press" and armaments manufacturers for seeking to stimulate war sentiment in the United States.[2]

The party could remain a pacifist island in a belligerent ocean because it was not subjected to the same historical pressures as its European counterparts. The question that faced European socialists in 1914 was whether they would side with their governments in an international crisis. The traditional antiwar position of comrades in the United States was subjected to no such point-blank demand. They were thousands of miles from the fighting. And while they probably would have followed the example of the European socialists in resisting invasion, actual or threatened, no such alternative was ever presented to them. In 1917, when their own country entered the war, no threat of foreign invasion was involved. American participation in the conflict entailed the sending of an expeditionary force to Europe.

On 7 April 1917, the day following the American declaration of war, an emergency national convention of the Socialist party opened in St. Louis, Missouri, to announce opposition to the action. The convention adopted an antiwar proclamation that was essentially a restatement of the classic Marxist analysis of war. Despite complaints on the part of a number of dissident Socialists that it should have been labeled the "near-treason resolution," the St. Louis proclamation received overwhelming support when submitted to a national referendum of the Socialist party membership.

Marcy's wholehearted support of her party's opposition to the carnage taking place across the Atlantic was expressed most clearly in articles and editorials written for the *International Socialist Review.* Four of these writings are reprinted here.

Notes

1. "Anti-War Manifestoes," *New Review* 2 (September 1914):523–24.
2. Alexander Trachtenberg, ed., *The American Socialists and the War* (New York: Rand School of Social Science, 1917), 10–17.

The Real Fatherland

What has "your" country ever done for you, Mr. Workingman? Has it been a real fatherland to you? Has it looked after your welfare? Has it given you the opportunity to have a warm home in the winter? Has it seen that you have clothing and food? Has it fed your children and assured them of sunshine and schooltime and playtime to fit them for the real work of life?

Are you a German, Frenchman or Englishman? Are you Russian, Austrian or Italian? Are you an American? It does not matter. This question applies to every workingman in the world. What has "your" country ever done for *you?*

Surely no one expects you to love a particular geographical district upon the face of the earth just because you happened to be born on it, unless that district has done something for you.

When you were a child, did your country throw protecting arms about you and feed and clothe and shelter you? Or did your working class father and mother have to struggle to give you a place to eat and sleep? Is there one spot in all "your" country where you may rest and live and sleep in peace without the weekly or monthly dig-up to a landlord? And if you have no money to pay rent and no work to earn money to pay rent, does "your" country come to your assistance and give you work or does "your" country send around a sheriff or some other city official to set you out in the snow and another official to drive you from the city with a club, a gun and a "move on"?

When you are unable to secure a job and are driven across country by the police of "your" country or the gendarmes until you find yourself on "foreign" soil, you will find native workers of that "foreign" land in the same predicament as your own. The Frenchman, the German, the Englishman are all driven from pillar to post, from city to city, because they have no jobs and no money to buy food and clothing and the right to live on the land of "their" country.

Patriotism means the love of the land in which you were born—that and nothing more. And why should you love that land any more than any other?

Mr. Workingman, what has your native land done for you that you should fight for her flag, her glory, or her power? No matter how large or powerful she may become, no matter how rich her resources and her natural wealth, you will share in none of these things unless you can find a boss to pay you money to spend. If you are rich, "your" country will open her arms to you and spread out her army, her laws, her police to

International Socialist Review 15 (September 1914): 177–78.

protect your riches. If you are penniless, she will just as readily drive you from her farthermost provinces or send you to vilest prisons.

"Your" country has protection only for the powerful, the rich, the idle; she has no care for those who are hungry, cold and sick. The flag of "your" nation is borne by the troops sent into districts where the hosts of poverty congregate, to drive them from the sight of the wealthy.

"Your" country has no place for you after you have built the railroads, harvested the crops, produced food and clothing for more than your own numbers. For when your work is done your pay ceases. All that you have made, all that you have produced, has been kept by your employers and you are turned out upon the mercies of "your" country in your old age, penniless and homeless, to starve.

Workingmen of the world, the land of your birth has done nothing for you. Conditions in Germany, France, Austria, England, Russia and America are practically the same. Everywhere you will find the workers earning barely enough to live on. Everywhere you will find thousands of men hunting jobs and no jobs. Everywhere you will find the rich protected and the poor driven out.

You have no country! Every national flag in the world today means protection for the employing class, who appropriate the things produced by the workers. It has no message for those who toil.

There is only one flag worth fighting for and that is the red flag, which means universal brotherhood of the workers of the world in their fight to abolish the profit system.

The real fatherland will cherish every one of its children. It will see that all have equality of opportunity and a chance to produce and procure all the good things of life. The real fatherland means a childhood free from work and worry for us all; useful work for every able-bodied man and woman; it means his product for the worker without profit to any boss; it means leisure and a regular old age income in the winter of life!

This is the real fatherland and this is Socialism!

International Capital and the World Trust

Today the greatest capitalist groups of the strongest nations in Europe are engaged in fighting for new worlds to conquer—capitalistically. No matter how this war terminates, and the next war ends, and the wars still following close upon their heels may happen to close, it is pretty certain that there will arise out of the world anguish and industrial disaster, one strong capitalist group dominating the world.

We are seeing the battle of the various big national Trusts being fought out before our eyes today, just as our fathers witnessed the fights of the warring steel kings and oil companies and railroad corporations only a few years ago in many modern countries.

And while some of our fathers, who may have been Socialists, realized that centralization, or the Trust, was a step forward in human progress, predicating, as it does, the time when the workers of the world shall take over these trusts to run them for the benefit of the working, instead of the exploiting class, while some of our fathers may have understood these things, they did nothing to HELP Rockefeller or Morgan or Harriman . . . in their great campaign for crushing out their competitors.

These were battles of the owning, capitalist class, and no intelligent workingman came forward to offer his life to help Rockefeller freeze out the independent oil companies. Men did not shoulder guns to give Morgan a monopoly of the American steel industry.

But in the fight of the German monopolies against French monopolies, of German trusts against English and Belgian trusts, the European workers have taken up arms and are today fighting the great war which will determine which national trust shall be master, which capitalist group shall dominate all Europe and, finally perhaps, the whole world.

Understanding these things, the revolutionary workers are opposed to fighting this war of their exploiters, for the benefit of their exploiters. They know that it will merely benefit the strongest capitalists of one great nation, that it will mean greater centralization and internationalization of capital.

And this is what all wars mean, except the class war (between the working class and those who rob them). And this is why we are opposed to ALL capitalist wars.

It is true that we may not be able to prevent these wars, but at least we must do all in our united power to prevent them. It is true that the internationalization of capitalism and the world trust may be inevitable, but it is equally true that we should vote no war funds, appropriations for increasing armies and navies to help along this gigantic centralization.

It should be the part of every intelligent workingman and woman, and every revolutionist in particular, to oppose and point out how these wars are prepared for and how the working class is used to fight and murder and die, solely in the interest of the great capitalists of the warring nations.

We should oppose all wars at the same time we are pointing out that they *are* the wars of the enemies of the working class, who are only seeking greater fields in which to exploit labor.

We must keep our hands clean from the responsibility of helping to wage or to make possible capitalist wars. We must oppose all war plans, whether it be for a small army or a large army, for a small navy or for enormous sea power. Of the greater or lesser evils we must choose NEITHER.

If the great capitalists of the various nations desire to fight for world conquest and world power, it may be that we cannot prevent them. But we can refuse to do their fighting for them.

Many well informed European comrades and scholars predict that this is only the first of a series of great world wars—that the capitalists of the great nations will bring about in their struggles to become the world-dominating capitalist group. This may well prove possible. But during these wars the workers who fight them may be either learning to perceive the interests instigating these great slaughters and to rebel as they understand, or they may degenerate into mere cogs in vast military machines, who know only enough to obey the orders of those in command.

Wars may be made the greatest educational force the world has ever known, provided we do not hesitate to point out the true causes and hidden interests behind them, provided we do not hesitate to show the workers where they are fighting the battles of their enemies, provided indeed, that we seize our opportunities for teaching the workers the real meaning of wars.

We must try to prevent these wars, and if we fail, use them so that they will be eye-openers to the working class, so that year by year, more and ever more, workers may understand the old double-cross system by which the worker loses, no matter which national capitalist group may win.

Mass Action: Where We Stand

. . . In spite of the fact that real socialists everywhere agree that all nationalist wars are waged in the interests of the capitalist classes, both offensive wars and so-called defensive wars, we have, here in America, as well as in the warring nations of Europe, so-called socialists who vote for war appropriations, for armies, who write editorials saying that the Socialist Party ought to assent to the invasion of Mexico; . . . we have so-called socialists endorsing plans for universal military service.

On the other hand, in the Socialist Party Platform of 1916, we have the

International Socialist Review 17 (December 1916): 367–69.

members of the American Socialist Party taking a stand for *mass action* and the *general strike* as a means to prevent war:

"The proletariat of the world has but one enemy, the capitalist class, whether at home or abroad. We must refuse to put into the hands of this enemy an armed force even under the guise of a 'democratic army,' as the workers of Australia and Switzerland have done.

"Therefore the Socialist Party stands opposed to military prepared-ness, to any appropriations of men or money for war or militarism. . . . The Socialist Party stands committed to the class war, and urges upon the workers in the mines and forests, on the railways and ships, in factories and fields, the use of their economic and industrial power, by refusing to mine the coal, to transport soldiers, to furnish food or other supplies for military purposes, and thus keep out of the hands of the ruling class the control of armed forces and economic power, necessary for aggression abroad and industrial despotism at home."

So we have the Socialist Party of American advocating *mass action* and the *general strike* to prevent war, as the Left Wing European Socialists are doing. It remains for us now to utilize this weapon at every opportunity as a means of *class protest, class revolt* against the degrading conditions imposed by wage slavery, and as a weapon to further the revolutionary movement. . . .

It is obvious to any revolutionist that socialist parties which restrict themselves to legislative contests alone are in no position to rally to the support of the working class in any sudden emergency. Left wing Euro-pean and American socialists expect that we American revolutionists will follow the lead of our comrades across the water, who have seen the suicidal folly of the old party tactics in the presence of a declaration of war of one nation upon another nation.

Furthermore, *mass action* is bound to become, is already in this country becoming the best school for revolutionary activity. As Marx taught, ideas do not fall from heaven, but spring from the actual, material *needs* of human beings. The same rule applies to *tactics* in a revolutionary movement; they follow in response to an obvious need. Furthermore, we have seen among the old so-called Marxian socialists of Europe how futile are mere *ideas* in the minds of leaders and of privates when they have not grown step by step with revolutionary *activity*.

The day of the leader in the revolutionary movement is past, for capitalist governments have everywhere discovered that where a constit-uency merely follows the dictates of socialists in office, or socialists editing periodicals, it is an easy matter to suppress the offensive press and imprison the leaders and check any incipient revolt. Mass action develops initiative in the rank and file and renders the working class independent of leaders.

The working class, schooled in Mass Action, cannot be suppressed or imprisoned, sold out or led astray. Further, Mass Action will develop new tactics, new weapons, new means for waging the class war for the abolition of the profit system.

We wish to send this message to our Left Wing comrades in war-torn France, and Belgium, in Germany, Russia and England, and to those loyal comrades in Holland fighting so valiantly for international working class solidarity:

We, too, in this class-war-torn Land of "Liberty," will do our small part in the great work you are doing to build up a true working class International that shall have for its aim the joining of the hands and hearts and heads and aims of the revolutionary workers of all lands for the overthrow of the Capitalist System of society.

We hereby wish to repudiate all so-called socialists, those traitors to the working class, whether they be at home or abroad, who march at the heads of military preparedness parades, who vote war appropriations, who advocate aggression on weaker nations, and sing the siren song of Nationalism as opposed to Internationalism.

The interests of the Mexican workers, the American, German, French, English, Belgian, Austrian workers, of all those who are exploited by the capitalist owners of the means of production—the interests of these people are *one*. These workers have no national flag, no country. They must unite against the capitalists of all nations and take back the world for those who labor and those who produce. They must unite to make the whole world the country of the workers of the world. . . .

The REVIEW stands for Political Action in its broadest sense, Mass Action, Industrial Unionism, Class Unionism and for International Socialism, of which these are the strongest weapons. We oppose Imperialism in all its forms.

We are for such reforms as shorter hours and higher wages only for the reason that the struggles of the workers for these things are one of the best means of education in the class struggle. No reforms can materially benefit the working *class* as long as the present system of *producttaking* continues.

Our Gains in War

We doubt whether Socialists and industrial unionists are ever going to *start* a revolution. This is not the way revolutions or even revolts arise.

International Socialist Review 17 (May 1917): 650–52.

First, we are too few in number; second, we cannot *plan* a revolution, and third, people do not *act* in *unison* because their ideas are similar.

People *act* when they are hungry and cold, at a time when they are torn from their old moorings and thrust into new sets of conditions, a new environment; when they are jolted from their old habits and customs, when they *suffer*, in short; the *mass* revolt only when they *have to*.

We cannot *make* our opportunity, but we must keep up a constant work of education and organization and class struggles in order to be ready to take advantage of opportunity when it is presented to us. And we are almost inclined to believe that such an opportunity may only come during some great cataclysm like the world war, or some other great national or international disaster when social institutions are crumbling and men and women are torn from their old habits of thought and of action, and Misery, Hunger and Death stalk abroad among the working class.

Every true Socialist opposes capitalist wars at all times with every ounce of his strength, by all means at his command—because such wars are waged in the interests of Big Business—to gain new territory for capitalist exploitation, or to save old fields to their capitalist possessors, to protect commerce, property or profits rather than human lives.

For if it were lives with which the governments of the world were concerned, you would find the government of the United States making war upon the railroads to save the lives of the thousands of railroad workers killed needlessly every year, or the German government making war against the landlords in Berlin to crush out the awful scourge of tuberculosis that has raged for years in that metropolis, or you would find the British government using its power to prevent famine in India and the chronic starvation that existed among the poor of England before the war.

We oppose capitalist wars because we know that, in the past, wars have brought in their train oppressive measures which have deprived the working class of freedom of the press, free speech, the right to organize and to strike, and the right of assembly. During war the working class *may* lose all the small gains they have made to better their conditions during the past fifty years at so much cost and sacrifice.

We oppose capitalist wars because they are *usually* the great foes of liberalism and democracy; because, when Imperialism has been saddled upon a nation, and a strong military caste stands ready to serve the billionaire owning class, we feel that it will be almost impossible for the productive workers of that nation to make any headway against the encroachments of capital. For the army may stand ready to break every strike; to suppress every tendency toward freedom; to crush out all revolt. . . .

In any nation, as war progresses and grows more intense, gradually the utterly useless parasites upon the social body are forced from their snug hiding places and set to work carrying on the task of feeding and clothing the people of that country, and the soldiers on the field.

Gradually production and distribution break away from all individual control and restraint and become social or national in scope. Every healthy human being is forced to perform some function in the social body in order to preserve what the publicists are pleased to call "their honor" or "their national unity." Meanwhile the old order is surely tumbling about their ears nevermore to be raised up again.

We are not so much concerned whether the border of this country, or of that country, be moved a few miles east or west, as we are in the changed methods of production and distribution, the economic changes—that emerge out of the war chaos, in the disappearance of institutions that have long served the exploiting classes so faithfully and so well. We are interested in learning that parliaments have become outworn, vestigial social organs, or institutions, no longer necessary to the social body.

We rejoice to see the people of Russia throw off the century old yoke of autocracy that has hampered her productive development, tho it be, in some measure, but to wage a sterner war.* We are glad to learn that some of England's underfed population are acquiring the habit of regular and abundant food, and still more happy over the news of a possible revolution that may forever destroy the Prussian military caste and bring some measure of gain to the working class of Germany.

Individuals have ceased to stand out in this war, which has grown to such colossal proportions that men are no longer big enough, important enough, to stand out in the noise of great social changes. The profit-mad capitalist classes of the various nations, who caused this war, are fighting, thru their home governments and armies, for new fields of profit-taking, or to preserve old fields of profit-making. And now that the war is on, they find that all things must yield to bring efficiency for the defeat of their competitors across the border lines.

Meanwhile their own national protective social institutions are tumbling about their ears and the rumblings of revolt and revolution are heard in nearly every land. During the war the first consideration of every government is to see that its soldiers are well clothed and well fed, and that its people are well housed and clothed and well fed, so that the people can supply the army. But what government (not planning great

---

*Following the overthrow of Tsar Nicholas II in February 1917, the new Provisional Government continued Russia's participation in the war. Russia withdrew from the conflict only after Lenin and the Bolsheviks seized power in October.

wars) concerns itself with the food, the shelter and the clothing of its people? Can we imagine that people who are becoming accustomed to regular work, regular pay, and, for the great portion of the population, a goodly measure of security—can we imagine that these people are going to permit themselves to be thrown into unemployment, uncertainty and hunger after the war is over?

Was it possible to break up the great trusts and monopolies once they were organized? Will it be possible to unscramble the industries absorbed by the governments during war time? We cannot believe it, for it is the *methods* of *production* which determine things, events and institutions, not the desires of the most powerful individuals.

If the war lasts long enough the new system of production may grow beyond the control of any individual or groups of individuals if *it has not already done so.*

You may wonder if so much that is good may come out of this great capitalist war, why we oppose this war, why we must oppose all capitalist wars with all our strength and all our means. We believe the answer is plain.

This is not *our* war—a war of the working class to throw off the yoke of exploitation. It is a war between great national and international capitalist groups to widen their spheres of profit-taking. . . .

We understand the game. We are not fooled, We see our own international working class interest. We will wage our own fight in *our own interests.* It is our mission to use the opportunity that may develop if the working class is driven to desperation by hunger and misery. It is our mission to gain from new opportunities things that will mean lasting economic independence and industrial democracy to the working class.

We believe this is the function of the advanced guard of the working class. Either these things or reaction will be the fruits of the war. . . .

10

The Need for Action

LONG before joining the IWW in 1918, Mary Marcy was a staunch supporter of industrial unionism and had little use for "parlor socialists" who substituted words for deeds. As early as 1909, when a well-known college professor from Ohio criticized the *International Socialist Review* for approving the methods used by workers in a successful strike at McKees Rocks, Pennsylvania, Marcy responded with a bluntly worded article in the IWW weekly *Solidarity* denouncing him as "long on theories and short on knowledge of practical action. . . . Organization is the one thing about which he knows least. But what he lacks in knowledge he makes up for in presumption. Knowing nothing he desires to lead." Together with "fat salaried editors" and other "ladylike men" who are wholly ignorant of "the real struggle," Marcy complained, "the college professor regards a strike in the light of a Pink Tea or an Ethical Culture Society Meeting."[1]

From Marcy's vantage point, it was not through theoretical expositions and polite debates that the interests of the workers were best served, but rather through organization and practical action. As she affirmed in "A Straw Man," an editorial appearing in the *International Socialist Review* of March 1913, "*Our* concern is the great class war. And the main things are: No compromise on the political field, and revolutionary class unionism on the economic field! Agitate! Educate! Organize!"[2]

The first five selections that follow reveal in unmistakable fashion Marcy's commitment to the revolutionary class unionism espoused by the IWW. The final selection combines a reaffirmation of her belief in the inevitability of a "socialized world" with a pointed attack on Emma Goldman's disillusionment with Soviet communism.

Once called "Red Emma" and the "mother of anarchy in America," Goldman was among the most active and audacious rebels of her time. A leading feminist, a pioneer advocate of birth control, and a sharp critic of capitalism, militarism, and government, she provoked extremes of adulation and criticism. Eugene Debs described her as "one of the sincerest women" he knew, and the *Nation* asserted in 1922 that her name should be on any list of the twelve greatest living American women. By way of contrast, J. Edgar Hoover denounced her as one of the "most dangerous radicals in this country," and an angry mob in San Diego, California, once threatened to "strip her naked" and "tear out her guts."[3]

Born in Kovno, Russia (Kaunas in modern Lithuania), in 1869, Goldman emigrated to the United States at age sixteen and settled in Rochester, New York. By 1889 she had espoused anarchism and had moved to New York City where she became associated with the émigré Russian revolutionist Alexander Berkman and with Johann Most, editor of the anarchist paper *Die Freiheit*. During the next several decades, she took part in strikes, waged numerous fights for free speech, raised funds for the IWW, published the anarchist magazine *Mother Earth* (1906–17), and toured the country lecturing on subjects ranging from Ibsen to birth control to the evils of religion. One of the few immigrant radicals who resisted a narrowly economic interpretation of social injustice and who stressed sexual, psychological, and cultural issues, she rejected socialist demands for state social welfare programs and for nationalization of major industries on the grounds that such innovations would only increase the power of government. She also actively urged people not to vote or hold any positions in government.

In 1919, after spending twenty months in prison for opposing the draft during World War I, Goldman was deported to Russia, where she remained until the end of 1921. Although she had been one of the first and most passionate defenders of the Bolshevik Revolution, she was soon disillusioned by the increasing concentration of power in the hands of the Soviet bureaucracy and the suppression of dissent. Her book *My Disillusionment in Russia* (1925) remains the best analysis by an anarchist of the revolution's failure.

After leaving Russia, Goldman remained active as a lecturer and writer in exile, mainly in England, Canada, France, and Spain. A staunch defender of the anarchists during the Spanish Civil War, she died in 1940 in Canada, where she had gone the year before in a last-minute effort to raise funds for the Catalonian revolutionists.

Notes

1. "Ladylike Men," *Solidarity*, 18 December 1909.
2. "A Straw Man," *International Socialist Review* 13 (March 1913): 691.
3. David Karsner, *Talks with Debs in Terre Haute (and Letters from Lindlahr)* (New York: New York Call, 1922), 69; *Nation* 114 (21 June 1922): 739; Hoover as quoted in Richard Drinnon, *Rebel in Paradise* (Chicago: University of Chicago Press, 1961), 215; Philip S. Foner, *History of the Labor Movement in the United States*, vol. 3, *The Industrial Workers of the World, 1905–1917* (New York: International Publishers, 1965), 201.

The Value of Immorality

The working class is kept in a condition of wage slavery through its HABITS of MORALITY. If, from childhood, in the home and in the school, in the shop or in the factory, we had not been restrained from following out our natural instincts, if we had not been steadfastly repressed and the morality of the master class carefully drilled into us and FORCED upon us in our daily CONDUCT as something desirable, we would today shake off the bonds that hold us in subjection and overthrow the profit system. It is our HABITS that keep us from revolting today—our MORAL HABITS.

Today Poverty cries to the high heavens the need of a new social order. All that stands between us and the things WE have PRODUCED, the houses we have built and do not occupy, the clothing we have made, the food we have produced, which we may not eat—all that separates us from these things, that belong to us, is our habits of inertia, INACTION, our *habit* of thinking and ACTING according to the morality that the employing class wants and teaches. And this moral conduct makes those who MAKE things the slaves of those who TAKE things.

If the whole working class had stepped out into society from a page in the life of our primitive ancestors, the very first thing they would do would be to satisfy their natural appetites for food, clothing, shelter and leisure. They would TAKE what they needed and the idle would be powerless to prevent them.

Of course, it is equally true that these savages would not have attained the class consciousness so necessary to their permanent control of industry, and which comes only from actual experience in modern industry, to make such a supremacy *lasting,*

It is the HABITS of morality, the HABIT of acting in the way the employing class calls "good" that keeps hungry men and women today from acting just as savages would act.

The need for working class control of industry is here. We have only to develop a new working class HABIT OF ACTION, a working class ethic, to make an end of a system that means unemployment, starvation and poverty to the workers of the world.

Consider the morals that are taught us from the cradle to the grave; the morals that are sung in the home and Sunday School, that we copy at school, that ring from press and pulpit, that the rich and respectable are always mouthing. All are in praise of ACTION or conduct that means safety and power and property to the rich and respectable because these actions, this kind of conduct makes unresisting slaves of the working class.

International Socialist Review 15 (March 1915): 528–29.

Now, morals have to do with "good" actions and "bad" actions; "good" conduct and "bad" conduct. And we have been carefully driven, coaxed and coerced into acting for what is "good" for the master class and is "bad" for US. We are so moral that we crawl under the sidewalks to freeze or starve to death before empty flats or bursting groceries; we are so courageous and "patriotic" that we die on the battlefields so that our employers may have newer and bigger markets; we are so industrious that we work overtime and put our brothers out of a job. . . .

Isn't it about time that we found a new line of CONDUCT, a new way of ACTING and LIVING that is more in harmony with OUR OWN INTERESTS?

Man's instincts still rule the world. The majority of us will ACT, will break all the moral and legal laws in order to preserve life in spite of any false *ideas* of "right" and "wrong." On this human instinct-to-live do we base our faith in the final triumph of the working class. It does not so much matter what a man THINKS, so long as his stomach, his needs and his ACTIONS are with us. What is really of importance in the class struggle is CONDUCT, how we ACT. Remember that it is OLD HABITS that keep us from revolting today. Men's ideas soon change when they ACT with us for our mutual interests. . . .

Every boss will tell you that obedience is a great virtue. It is a virtue in slaves only. The man who is thoroughly disciplined into HABITS of obedience is the man who starves to death in the very city where he has made ten thousand loaves of bread.

Drug habits are "bad" for all men, but they are not half so fatal to working class emancipation as the moral slave HABIT of OBEDIENCE.

In your daily actions, remember that the boss wants his slaves to possess habits of discipline and obedience, national spirit and courage (to die for HIS interests).

The Revolution wants men and women with *habits* of INITIATIVE, men of international class solidarity, of courage to fight the class that robs us. . . .

The boss loves a humble worker who is economical and saves his money against a period of unemployment. The worker who respects authority, is contented and loyal (to the interests of the boss) will never become an active rebel. He is sure to work longer hours at a low wage scale.

If temperate he can live on lower wages. He is the logical lick-spittle, stool pigeon, and scab. And the preachers assure him that he is "laying up treasures" for himself in Heaven, "where moth and rust do not corrupt nor thieves break through and steal."

Beware of the man whom the boss calls a model worker. His moral conduct, his virtuous activities will prevent his ever becoming a real factor in the working class revolution.

What we need is MORE REBELLION, new habits of fighting the capitalist system, independence and initiative in organizing the workers.

The only morality, the only kind of ACTION with which the revolutionary movement is concerned is LOYALTY TO THE INTERESTS OF THE WORKING CLASS!

Why the Socialists Must "Harp On" the Class Struggle

Somebody said, "Let's stop talking about class struggle," and somebody said, "Let's." And then the Innocent Bystander inquired, "What IS the class struggle?"

That is the question: What IS the CLASS STRUGGLE?

It is the struggle between workers and the bosses for the things produced BY the WORKERS. It would be as easy to stop talking about the class struggle as it would be to stop talking about food and rent and marriage and death and disease—for the class struggle is intermingled with all of these things.

The working class produced all the commodities existing in the world today; all the food, houses, street cars, railroads, all of the clothing. All the coal has been dug by workers, the lumber has been cut and hauled by the workers, the food has been planted and raised and cooked by the workers.

But the class struggle arises over the fact that employers of labor appropriate all these things produced by the workers. These employers pay the workers who produce all these commodities miserable wages, while they, who produce nothing, keep our commodities. . . .

The whole life of the working class is determined by what portion of the value of his produce he receives. If he can force the coal operator to give him $6 out of the $18 worth of coal he has dug, it is obvious that the miner can change his whole mode of life from what it was when he received only $3 a day in wages.

He can live in a better house, buy better food, afford to get married and wear better clothes. When his children are sick he can engage a good doctor and buy medicine. His whole life depends upon just how much he gets out of the coal he digs.

The class struggle is the most important thing in the life of the

---

Northwest Worker, 4 November 1915. The *Northwest Worker* was an IWW weekly published in Everett, Washington.

working class today. We could not stop talking about it if we wanted to. Every time we ask for more wages and the boss feels that he has to give them to us, we have gained a little bit more of the value we have produced, and we have left a lower dividend for the boss. We have fought the small part of the class struggle.

The bosses want low wages and long hours because they know that low wages and long hours mean more surplus value (for more profits) for them. Every workingman and woman wants higher wages and shorter hours, although they know this will leave smaller dividends for their employers.

The class struggle is the struggle of the whole working class with the owning class for more of, and finally all of, the value of the things it produces. It is a struggle because the capitalist class opposes all these benefits for the workers, higher wages and shorter hours, with all its power. The capitalist class knows that when the workers organize and unite to keep the entire value of the things they make, there will be no more profits for the exploiters of labor.

The sort of things that are taught in the colleges, schools, and universities are determined by the class struggle; the rich and owning class insists that pupils and students shall be taught to be honest, contented, hard-working, humble, wage-workers—so that even education is a part of the class struggle. But education represents the interests of the owning class just so far as the owning class can control the educational institutions of the country. . . .

Every social institution, even when it is supposed to be "free" as it is in this country, represents the interests of one of the two opposing sides in the class struggle. Take the church, the state, or the government; the laws, judges, police, the army and navy; the schools and the press— nearly all these represent the class that TAKES the thing which the workers MAKE.

Nearly all Socialist and labor periodicals, particularly the industrial union periodicals, try to represent only the working class in its struggle for more of the products and finally to abolish the wage system and to give the workers the entire value produced by the workers.

About the only way the workers can get anything from the bosses today is by organizing with other workers. Up to a few years ago much of the struggling between the owning class and the working class was entirely on the question of more wages or less wages, longer or shorter hours. But now the workers in every "civilized" country in the world are beginning to agitate and educate and organize the workers of the whole world to carry on a gigantic struggle against the capitalist or owning class—not for shorter hours and higher wages—not for more of the things produced by the workers, to be owned by the workers, but in order to take the great manufacturing plants and producing plants and factories, the mines, mills and lands for the workers, so that the workers of the world, and only the workers, may receive the full value of the things they produce.

This is the Class Struggle on which is based every labor and Socialist movement worthy of the name today.

Nobody likes the Class Struggle. Every intelligent man and woman in the world today regrets that there is raging everywhere such a mighty class war.

Sometimes in some countries those who rob the workers can fool and force and deceive them into fighting battles for the owning class by pretending that a war will prove of benefit to the working class of that country. but when these wars are over the workers always find that the bosses have deceived them. They find that they are still forced to make all the useful and beautiful things used by mankind while the owning class continues to take these things, for which it pays the workers only the lowest possible wage.

And then, very gradually, the workers begin to wake up and to join hands again with their robbed and exploited comrades across the national boundary lines. Then they begin to learn the meaning of "Workers of the World, Unite. You have nothing to lose but your chains."

The Fighting Instinct

Some people believe that Organization is the greatest thing in the world. They point to the German military organization to prove their contention. They refer to the German Social Democracy. But we do not agree with them.

Organization, unless it *does* something—unless it *acts*, means nothing. Perhaps man's natural tendency to *fight* is the greatest of all his heritages. Some of us see this. We know that it is man's natural tendency to satisfy his hunger, to seek shelter, and to perpetuate the species. But he has to fight for an opportunity to do these things.

From savagery to civilization it has been the tribes, and later, the nations, which have known how to *fight* that have survived. The weak and peaceful tribes met the strong and warlike hordes and were annihilated.

International Socialist Review 16 (January 1916): 433–34.

And the old law holds good today even as it did a hundred thousand years ago; the weak man, the peaceful man, goes down in the struggle and the strong survive.

The strong continue to take from the weak and grow stronger with every theft, for men learn to fight, *by fighting,* and men grow strong *to* fight, by fighting.

Civilized man today is governed almost as much by the things he has *learned* and the *habits* he has formed, as by his natural instincts and tendencies. Our natural instinct, when we are hungry, is to satisfy that hunger—and yet hundreds of thousands of starving men and women pass and repass every day, wagon loads, and train loads, of food which they do not touch.

The *habit* of respecting Private Property in them has grown stronger than the old instinct to eat and to live. Historically, it has been only recently that man learned to work, to apply himself for hours at a time to any given task. He did not take naturally to work. His instincts were all against application. And yet we see some people so far losing this instinct for idleness and for play that they actually beg to be allowed to perform work in their old age that they had rebelled against and loathed in their youth.

Most of man's original tendencies, or instincts, serve to preserve the human race. But these instincts may become so suppressed in childhood and in youth by the long and painful efforts of their parents, teachers and employers, as well as their governments, that some of them cease to function.

Habit may become so fixed that it will prove even stronger than the instinct to eat when we are hungry; this is why hundreds of thousands of people go about in a semi-starved condition from one year's end to another.

The working class of the world is increasingly exploited by the owning classes. And man's *original* tendency today is to fight over the *food,* the *clothing,* etc., etc., just as primitive men fought for the results of the chase centuries ago.

And the owning class, or capitalist class, is today fighting for more and ever more of the things produced by the workers. The Class Struggle is the every-day struggle of the workers and the idlers *for the products,* of the workers.

The capitalist, or owning class, is appropriating these things today. Who is going to have them tomorrow?

We believe the class that fights most steadily. For as soon as the workers pause to rest, cease to fight and to demand more and ever more of their products, or the value of their products, the stronger grows the capitalist class.

And every time the capitalist class grows lazy or careless, the workers will, if they continue to fight, gain more of the things they make.

Peaceful habits, in their association with the capitalist or employing class, will mean lower wages, longer hours, more abject slavery for the workers. Fighting habits, habits of rebellion, among the working class will mean *more strength* to fight, more *wisdom* on *how to fight,* more *desire* to fight—the capitalist system which robs them.

Some of us love the rare, nice little boys who refuse to fight when they are playing. We reward these boys with candy and words of praise; and we punish the children who *fight.* This is the general attitude of parents today. This is the attitude of teachers today. We punish those who possess the fighting spirit when we should reward or encourage them.

Boys are young fighting animals and we may either start the long period of suppression of this natural and vital instinct in their early years or encourage it.

The thing we should do is to teach our children and the youths about us, and the working class in general everywhere, to fight in their *own interest;* we should show them that to fight in their own interest means to fight the present *profit system.*

The instinct to *fight* for what we need is what the working class must encourage today and tomorrow, and the next day. We shall never get anything from the exploiting class unless we fight for it. When we have the intelligence to fight unitedly, and only then, can we ever hope to win a victory over the capitalist class.

As long as we only go about whining, and *talking* and regretting the condition of the working class, we shall never gain one foot of ground against our exploiters. Every time we *rebel* and *fight* for more of the things we produce, we learn new ways for more effective fighting, we become better prepared to meet the next attack of the enemy.

Every time we meekly permit a further encroachment by the employing class we are building up habits of submission that will be all the more difficult to overcome when we do engage the enemy.

It is not today the capitalist class that holds the working class of the world in subjection, but the habits of inaction, of turning the other cheek, of submission on the part of the workers themselves.

The capitalist class exploits you because you have not fought often enough, hard enough nor regularly enough to learn *how* to fight. And they are going to keep right on exploiting you until you become a great worldwide fighting organization of the working class. And remember—

An ounce of fighting rebellion today will mean a pound of revolt tomorrow.

The Power of Labor

Whenever we marvel at the power possessed by the working class, we are struck by the poverty, suffering, and endurance of the workers.

We know that all the useful and beautiful commodities in the world are the products of their hands. We know the toilers have built every ship, have constructed bridges to span the rivers, have wrought giant locomotives and great trains to carry the food and clothing and machinery produced by the laborers all over the face of the globe.

We look about in the big cities and see everywhere the products of the hands of labor. And when we go down into the slums we find the workers, who build mansions, palaces, luxurious apartment houses, skyscrapers, living there in poverty and uncertainty.

We see our comrades, who produce food for the whole world, living upon the poorest and cheapest foods. They are underfed and their children undernourished.

We find our fellow workers, who raise cotton, wool, silk, and who make clothing for all men and women, wearing rags, or clothed in shoddy.

And yet—the productive and necessary workers are so powerful that they can blight the largest cities with famine within a week. So powerful are they that they can fold their arms and bring starvation upon the Leisure Classes who live by the labor of others.

Upon the shoulders of the productive and the necessary workers rests the whole life of Society. Without these workers no man eats, nor is warmed, is clothed, travels about, has shelter from the storm and the cold.

These workers possess the economic power of life and death over all men. And yet—

These men sleep in tenements, suffer hunger and cold.

It is your labor, O workers, which has made other men, idle men, secure. And for you there is no security. You, who have builded palaces, are without homes.

You, who have packed the storehouses with clothing, who have garbed whole nations, are sorely put to it to provide the overalls you need to labor in.

You productive workers! You turn all wheels and cause cities to spring up, and peoples to eat. Engines leap at the touch of your fingers; whistles blow; cars run; wheels revolve; the World awakes!

You have fed the world; clothed and warmed the human race and when you fold your arms, when the workers in a whole industry fold

---

From *The Right to Strike* (Chicago: Charles H. Kerr & Co., n.d.), 23–25.

their arms, when all the workers fold their arms, all these good things must cease.

The preachers tell us to be satisfied with the lowly station into which it has pleased their gods to place us. But our station is not lowly; the basis of great power lies in our calloused hands, for, when we, the working class fold our arms—

> The source of the food supply is dried,
> There is no longer clothing,
> Nor coal, neither trains, nor travel, nor
>   steaming ships!
> When we, the workers, fold our arms!
>
> Machines are hushed;
> In the cities there is neither
> Heat nor light; neither water nor gas;
> Neither food nor coal;
> When we, the workers, fold our arms!

And we rejoice in the power which is ours. We are glad of our strength and our brains to produce things that people may live in comfort; may eat and be merry; may travel and work and live and love!

Glad are we also that, organized, united as a class, with minds awake, we, the workers, possess the economic power to enforce whatsoever we need and desire and find right and workable in this world of men.

The world of men is a dark place, a hungry, thirsty, cold place, a sick, homeless, idle and dying world—without our labor. It is BY OUR LABOR that all good things come to mankind.

And it is by OUR ECONOMIC POWER that we shall some day make this a world in which all strong men and strong women shall give labor for labor and service for service; and none shall share who does not also contribute to society.

In the meantime the STRIKE is one of the greatest weapons by which we workers can secure a greater portion of the value we create, and it is what we need in our efforts to resist FURTHER EXPLOITATION. . . .

Only One Way

There is only one way to economic security and hope and happiness for the working class. And that is the way the Industrial Workers of the World of America have always advocated.

Industrial Solidarity, 23 December 1922. This unqualified endorsement of the IWW was found in Marcy's effects by her husband and published posthumously. *Industrial Solidarity* was an IWW weekly published in Chicago. Prior to 10 September 1921 it was named first *Solidarity* and later *Defense News Bulletin.*

We do not mean by this that all the workers of Germany, England, France, America, Japan, Russia, etc. etc., will have to join the American IWW before they can abolish capitalism. But we do mean that they will have to take the IWW WAY to a NEW society OF and for the workers—(a communist society, if you choose to call it that, by which we mean a society in which all healthy men and women will perform some necessary labor and in which their products will be poured forth in such a torrent through the use of the most modern machinery and electric power that men and women can, out of their own great plenty, be able to use all they need and desire.)

It does not particularly matter what the groups of workers in any of these countries may call themselves. The IWW has blazed the way. It has always demanded, and in spite of foes and "friends," still demands, that the workers on the job shall work out their own salvation; that the forward, revolutionary movement must be OF, BY and FOR the workers themselves.

There is no other way—ultimately. No matter what route the workers may be forced to take temporarily through necessity in other countries when capitalism collapses—perhaps before it is ripe, in a modern capitalist country, like America, the INDUSTRIAL WORKERS ALONE must lead the way. . . .

The industrial proletariat is the most advanced class, historically, in all capitalist countries. It is most numerous in America in proportion to the whole population. It is the most class conscious. It knows most about carrying on industry. It is the only class that CAN carry on production. It is the only class that can represent the proletariat.

The IWW has always claimed that the new society would split from the loins of a highly developed CAPITALIST society. Revolution at any time and at any place must almost completely disorganize production, because every ruling class prefers to pull down the whole of society rather than lose one bit of its power. It struggles till the last ditch. The social groups which then find themselves between both classes will after a time flock to the banner of the working class. They will not know the working class, nor what it can and must do.

Beware, Professionals!

If we are induced to give power to these professional groups, we will be betrayed, not because the individuals composing them are always traitors but because they will not understand the needs of the new society. They will not understand the working class.

If given office these groups will form a body of professional jobholders—divorced from industry who will become capitalist retrogrades. They will delay the forward march of proletarian progress and will need, in turn, to be overthrown.

America is a highly developed capitalist country. Her wage working class is increasing in proportion to the population every day. What we need here is an educated, thinking, reasoning working class, or as many workers as possible in that class, who will be capable of organizing the rest of the workers to carry on production WITHOUT PROFIT, for the working class.

Recent historical developments show these things plainly. The new society must spring from a wage working class which is the product of a highly developed capitalism. The workers in it must be class conscious, organized. The wage workers in an economically backward country cannot be numerically strong enough, sufficiently class conscious, to leap from feudalism into a society organized for the whole working class.

Class consciousness is developed through class *action,* and only incidentally from books.

The IWW was always right. Events are proving this. What we need in America is more organization, more action, more education (for those who do the acting), a closer knowledge of the revolutionary movement in other countries, so that we may benefit by some of their great successes, and avoid their mistakes.

Emma Goldman and the Soviets

From more than one source it has reached our ears that Emma Goldman is not at all satisfied with Soviet Russia and that she yearns for the good old days in America before the war when bored society ladies derived a thrill from hearing her discuss sex problems and advocate "Free love" with the lid off. In those affluent times a lady who disliked to soil her hands with the drudgery of honest toil could always be assured of a group of gushing satellites who were willing to pay for the privilege of being entertained.

We knew perfectly well when Emma was deported to Russia that she was not going to like it there. For she never did understand the laws underlying historical progress, nor the economic structure of society, nor the evolutionary trend of society. And she had about as much real use for the working class as John D. Rockefeller. . . .

She does not understand what has happened during the past five years

---

Toiler, 2 July 1920. The *Toiler* was a weekly published in Cleveland, Ohio, from 26 November 1919 until 28 January 1922. It succeeded the *Ohio Socialist* and announced first that it was the publication of the Communist Labor Party of Ohio and later simply that it was "published by the Toiler Publishing Association."

nor what is transpiring in the world today. She does not really want a workers' revolution, and she says that industrial communism is tyranny. The conditions of everybody are too leveled up, as it were. In fact after seeing Soviet Russia during war-time, when the Russian people are compelled to sacrifice personal comfort and leisure and the Arts, in order to protect themselves from the armies of the capitalist countries of the whole world, her thoughts turn back longingly to the "good old days" that are never coming back, anywhere, anymore.

Emma Goldman does not know that we have had ANARCHY in production for the past seventy-five years and that all the conditions of hunger, war, despair, failures of the credit system, financial disasters are but the full fruits and blossoms of the sort of thing she prefers to Communism.

For many years in all the modern anarchistic, or capitalistic, countries we have had production begin and production cease solely at the dictates of a few owners of industry whose only thought was, NOT of the needs of society, but of whether industry yielded a sufficient quota of profits for their own personal appropriation. Shops opened and closed; railroads were built and operated or were permitted to fall into disuse, solely on the basis of whether or not they yielded sufficient profits to the capitalists.

And this anarchy in industry, in production and distribution, brought about the great war; killed off ten million young men and maimed ten million more; ravaged whole nations, and it is this anarchy, planlessness, individualism—run—mad that is to-day causing the collapse of the world's credit system; causing inflation and rising prices, that is choking off industry. It is anarchy or capitalism which is to-day unwillingly digging its own grave, destroying the foundation of the existing system and making revolution as inevitable as the stars in their courses.

It was anarchy in production and distribution and in finance that caused the collapse of the Czar's regime and that is causing the disintegration of the civilized world to-day—unbridled capitalist anarchy.

But Emma does not know that industry and production are anarchistic in Europe and in the United States, nor that the credit system has failed nor how the workers are exploited. She does not care that world-Capitalism is warring upon Russia and that in the face of the collapse of the old system the Russian workers have not had time to rebuild in peace but are forced to carry on their educational work and their great plans for socialized industry in the face of the combined capitalist armies of the world.

All that she seems to be interested in is the fact that in Russia people have lost their old time liberty of being able to graft off the ignorance of the people and that she is in a land where it is necessary to become a useful citizen or to go hungry.

There are several kinds of freedom that nobody is able to enjoy in

Russia to-day and this is precisely what has made Soviet Russia the target of all the reactionaries all over the world, from the millionaire owners of industry to the petty grafters who prey on society. To-day, provided you are a healthy man or woman, you eat according to the work you do, according to the service you perform. Everybody who is a useful member of society is allowed his share in the food and clothing and pay in Russia. But nobody any longer is free to live off the labor of others or by the exploitation of men and women in any manner whatsoever.

The coming days may be rather difficult; for the social parasites who do not understand the events of the times. They do not realize that CAPITALISM, or anarchy in production, has failed, and is bound to succumb in chaos and utter rout because of its own contradictions.

We are going to have world revolution, not because of the aims of any class, but because, through the failure of the capitalist credit system, capitalism is becoming unable to carry on production. The same money is deposited over and over again in the banks, and the bank deposits are increasing more than twenty times as fast as the gold supply. So that the banks are in a constant state of insolvency. They are no longer able to lend sufficient money to carry on business enterprises to maintain industry. They are compelled to curtail credit when the United States, for example, needs hundreds of millions of dollars to be expended in extending and rebuilding and improving the railroads alone. They need either to print more unbacked paper money or to hold more and more money in the banks to partially protect their depositors.

Industry is being CHOKED OFF by Capitalism, not by the revolutionists, and every student of history knows that when production ceases, the inevitable result is revolution in self-preservation for the mass of the people.

And when Anarchy, or Capitalism, brings CHAOS, nothing on earth will lift society out of the disaster but SOCIALIZED production and SOCIALIZED PLANNING. When it actually becomes impossible to produce for PROFITS, men and women will either have to starve to death or RESUME PRODUCTION on the basis of HUMAN USE AND HUMAN NEEDS.

And so the socialism of Marx and Engels is on its way. No matter whether you are glad or sorry, no matter whether you may be working for it, or die trying to prevent its coming, it is as certain as the approach of the seasons.

We are bound to have a socialized world, socialized production and distribution—not because we do or do not want it, but because Capitalism is going to leave the whole world high and dry in utter chaos. There is only ONE WAY OUT!

Mary Marcy's Published Writings

(*ISR* denotes *International Socialist Review.*)

Books and Pamphlets

A Free Union: A One Act Comedy of "Free Love." Chicago: Charles H. Kerr & Co., 1921.

How the Farmer Can Get His. Chicago: Charles H. Kerr & Co., 1916.

Industrial Autocracy. Chicago: Charles H. Kerr & Co., 1919. An excellent example of Marcy's efforts to educate the workers as to the nature of capitalism and its approaching collapse. Capitalist "autocracy" is described as having fostered prostitution, brought on increasing "poverty and despair to the *productive* Many," and filled the jails with those "who proposed democracy in industry." But "thanks to the contradictions in the capitalist system," Marcy affirms, "the system is itself collapsing over the whole world" and "what we intend to have in the very near future is not autocracy, but democracy in industry." It is the task of the workers "to exercise power" to force this change. "Nobody but yourselves is going to do anything for you now. You must organize industrially, as well as politically, and carry on the work of education as you have never done before."

Open the Factories. Chicago: Charles H. Kerr & Co., 1921.

Out of the Dump: A Story of Organized Charity. Chicago: Charles H. Kerr & Co., 1908.

Rhymes of Early Jungle Folk. Chicago: Charles H. Kerr & Co., 1922.

The Right to Strike. Chicago: Charles H. Kerr & Co., n.d.

Shop Talks on Economics. Chicago: Charles H. Kerr & Co., 1911.

Stories of the Cave People. Chicago: Charles H. Kerr & Co., 1917.

Why Catholic Workers Should Be Socialists. Chicago: Charles H. Kerr & Co., 1914.

Women as Sex Vendors, or Why Women Are Conservative (Being a View of the Economic Status of Women). Chicago: Charles H. Kerr & Co., 1918. This pamphlet was coauthored by Marcy's brother, Roscoe B. Tobias.

Articles, Leaflets, and Poems

"The Advancement of the Canning Industry." *International Socialist Review* 14 (December 1913):351–55.

"Are You a Socialist?" *ISR* 12 (August 1911):106–7.

"Auto Car Making." *ISR* 15 (January 1915):406–12.

"The Awakening of China." *ISR* 10 (January 1910):632–35. The first of several pieces Marcy wrote on the modernization of China.

"The Barbo Fair." *Industrial Pioneer* 1 (May 1923):5–6. Marcy's last article. Published posthumously in the successor to the IWW journal *One Big Union Monthly.*

"The Battle for Bread at Lawrence." *ISR* 12 (March 1912):533–43. A detailed discussion of the origins and aims of the massive Lawrence, Massachusetts, strike of textile workers organized by the IWW.

"Beginners' Course in Socialism and the Economics of Karl Marx." *ISR* 11 (November 1910):281–82; (December 1910):334–35; (January 1911):424–26; (February 1911):483–85; (March 1911):542–44; (April 1911):619–22; (May 1911):696–98; 12 (July 1911):37–39.

"Better Any Kind of Action than Inert Theory!" *ISR* 8 (February 1915):495–96. Marcy maintains that it is "the HABIT of taking orders, *of obedience,*" that has sent millions of soldiers to the battle fronts of Europe since August, 1914, and argues that without this habit of "mental inertia . . . the desires of the capitalist class for new conquests would have remained fruitless." It is the task of workers "everywhere and at all times" to do away with habits of obedience to both Kaiser and labor leader. "Better a thousand premature or futile strikes every year than a rank and file that moves only in obedience to the word of command from leaders."

"The Boys on the Grand Trunk." *ISR* 11 (September 1910):161–63. Points to the lessons to be drawn from a successful railroad workers strike in Michigan, among them that "the HINDUS, the NEGROES, the JAPANESE and CHINESE WORKINGMEN are our exploited comrades and that our common enemy is CAPITALISM."

"Breaking Up the Home." Chicago: Charles H. Kerr & Co., 1912. This illustrated leaflet is a revision of Marcy's article "One Hundred Years Ago," published in the June 1912 issue of the *ISR.* It describes household life in "grandmother's day" and relates what the invention of new machinery and the progress of specialized production have done to the old-fashioned home.

"The Busy Silkworm." *ISR* 12 (October 1911):222–26.

"Can a Socialist Serve 'All the People'?" *ISR* 12 (September 1911):150–51. Socialists elected to office who declare that they intend to "serve all the people," warns Marcy, "should be regarded with great suspicion, because nobody can serve capitalism and the working class at the same time."

"The Cause of Rising Prices." *ISR* 10 (March 1910):769–74.

"The Cause of War." *ISR* 18 (July 1917):28–29.

"Changing China." *ISR* 13 (January 1913):528–32.

"China and Standard Oil." *ISR* 14 (April 1914):594–96.

"The Class Struggle." *ISR* 16 (October 1915):206–8. A clearly written explanation of "the class struggle"—what it is and why it is necessary.

"The Class Struggle Disguised." *ISR* 17 (June 1917):751–52.

"Competing with the Machine." *ISR* 14 (January 1914):400–402.

"Direct Action." *ISR* 16 (September 1915):179–80.

"Economic Determinism." *Industrial Pioneer* 1 (September 1921):9–10.

"Economic Determinism and the Sacred Cows." *ISR* 10 (June 1910):1063–64. Marcy predicts that the sacred cattle of the Malay Peninsula will soon fall victim to the Beef Trust. "Before Economic Necessity all men bow. Kings abdicate; religions fade away; the Holy of Holies is eaten for lunch and Gods are harnessed to supply the need. Before Economic Necessity nothing is fixed. Nothing is evil. Nothing is sacred!"

"Economic Power." *ISR* 18 (February 1918):401–5. Marcy's final article in the *ISR*. The February 1918 issue was the journal's last.

"Efficiency the Test." *New York Call,* 8 May 1910.

"Emma Goldman and the Soviets." *Toiler,* 2 July 1920.

"The Fate of the College Graduate." In *Socialist Dialogues and Recitations,* compiled by Josephine R. Cole and Grace Silver. Chicago: Charles H. Kerr & Co., 1913, 57.

"A Felicitan Fair." *ISR* 6 (June 1906):729–30. Exploitation of labor is the theme of this fictional story, Marcy's first contribution to the *ISR* following "Letters of a Pork Packer's Stenographer."

"The Fighting 'Instinct.' " *ISR* 16 (January 1916):433–34.

"The Food Destroyers." *ISR* 14 (November 1913):267–68. A condemnation of the practice of destroying food as a means of driving up the price.

"The Germans in Turkey." *ISR* 13 (June 1913):871–74. Marcy maintains that Germany has found a more subtle way than military invasion to subjugate the foreigner. The Turkish government "is under absolute control of the German financiers who can compel it to obey German mandates at any and all times."

"German Socialists in Russia." *ISR* 18 (October 1917):216–17.

"The Goose and the Golden Egg." *ISR* 16 (February 1916):494–95. "The working class is the goose that lays the golden egg of profits for the factory owner and the mill owner today." When will the workers wake up, organize, and "shake off these parasites?"

"Hamstringing the Unions." *ISR* 17 (October 1916):226–27.

"Hard Times and How to Stop Them." *ISR* 13 (March 1913):654–55.

"The Hatfield Whitewash." *ISR* 14 (July 1913):54–55.

"Helen Keller's New Book." *ISR* 14 (December 1913):350. Marcy here praises Keller's *Out of the Dark.* From 1909 until 1921, when she decided that her chief life work was to be devoted to raising funds for the American Foundation for the Blind, Keller was an active participant in the American radical movement. She joined the Socialist Party of America and wrote and spoke actively in its behalf, was friendly to the IWW, defended the Bolshevik Revolution, and ardently championed the working class.

"Help for West Virginia." *ISR* 13 (June 1913):895.

"How Capitalists Solve the Problem of the Unemployed." *ISR* 14 (May 1914):648–50. A description of the brutal treatment accorded a band of unemployed drifters in Sacramento, California.

"How the Farmer Is Exploited." *ISR* 16 (March 1916):559–61.

"How Tom Saved the Business." *ISR* 9 (February 1909):598–602.

"If Socialism Came." In *Socialist Dialogues and Recitations,* compiled by Josephine R. Cole and Grace Silver. Chicago: Charles H. Kerr & Co., 1913, 55–56.

"International Capital and the World Trust." *ISR* 16 (October 1915):241–42.

Introduction to *Debs: His Life, Writings and Speeches; With a Department of Appreciations.* 3d ed. Chicago: Charles H. Kerr & Co., 1910.

"It's Up to You!" In *Socialist Dialogues and Recitations*, compiled by Josephine R. Cole and Grace Silver. Chicago: Charles H. Kerr & Co., 1913, 58–59.

"The IWW Convention." *Liberator* 2 (July 1919):10–12. A description of the work of the Eleventh IWW Convention in Chicago, May 1919. The *Liberator* (1918–24) was successor to the *Masses* (1911–17), a victim of government suppression during World War I.

"Killed Without Warning By the American Capitalist Class." *ISR* 17 (March 1917):519–22.

"Ladylike Men." *Solidarity*, 18 December 1909.

"Letters of a Pork Packer's Stenographer." *ISR* 5 (August 1904):102–9; (September 1904):175–78; (November 1904):296–303; (December 1904):363–69; (January 1905):418–23.

"Machines That Have Made History." *ISR* 15 (March 1915):530–36.

"The March of the Machine." *ISR* 14 (September 1913):147–49.

"Marxian Economics." *ISR* 17 (January 1917):418–20; (February 1917):489–91; (March 1917):552–54; (April 1917):621–24.

"Mass Action: Where We Stand." *ISR* 17 (December 1916):367–69.

"The Milwaukee Victory." *ISR* 10 (May 1910):991–92. Expressing her pleasure at the election of a Socialist mayor and city council in Milwaukee, Marcy urges further action: "The first great need of any organization is organization. Now is the time for the revolutionary unionists to get busy. . . ."

"A Month of Lawlessness." *ISR* 18 (Septebmer 1917):154–57. A denunciation of the forcible deportation of a thousand striking miners from Bisbee, Arizona, to the Hermanas Desert and the lynching of IWW leader Frank Little by six Montana "vigilantes."

"Morals and War Babies." *ISR* 15 (June 1915):719–23.

"Morals in Rubber." *ISR* 13 (December 1912):466–69.

"My God." In Jack Carney, *Mary Marcy*. Chicago: Charles H. Herr & Co., 1922, 13.

"The Near-Socialist." *ISR* 11 (October 1910):215–16. An imaginary conversation "overheard" between a small automobile manufacturer and a Socialist—"a molder by trade, who knows the economics of Karl Marx from A to Z." The manufacturer erroneously believes himself "a Near-Socialist," on the grounds that he wants "to eliminate graft, to put honest men in office and make rich men bear their just share of taxes." The molder sets him straight: "Socialists have just one great aim. This is the only thing that makes them and their movement different from other movements the world over. We mean to ABOLISH THE WAGE SYSTEM."

"The New York Garment Workers." *ISR* 13 (February 1913):583–88.

"The Night Before Christmas: A Monologue." *ISR* 10 (December 1909):490–93. This fictional piece dramatizing the plight of a department store clerk was reprinted in the Schenectady, Ohio, *Citizen*, 2 December 1910.

"Nine Sharpshooters." *ISR* 14 (February 1914):462–63. Marcy praises nine Colorado mine strikers—former army sharpshooters—who shot some machinegunners hired by the owners.

"One Big Union Wins at Lawrence." *ISR* 12 (April 1912):613–30. A detailed account of the Lawrence, Massachusetts, strike of textile workers, described by Marcy as "the greatest victory in American labor history." William D. Haywood and the IWW are featured prominently.

"One Hundred Years Ago." *ISR* 12 (June 1912):837–43.

"One Way of Trimming the Farmer." *ISR* 17 (July 1916):37–40.

"Only One Way." *Industrial Solidarity,* 23 December 1922.

"Open the Shops and Factories." *Industrial Pioneer* 1 (June 1921):19–21.

"Organize With the Unemployed." *ISR* 15 (September 1914):157–59. Employed workers are urged to aid their unemployed comrades, thus preventing employers from hiring the latter to keep down wages. "Remember that as soon as we begin to control the supply of workers . . . we can shorten hours and raise wages."

"Our Gains in War." *ISR* 17 (May 1917):650–52.

"Our Real Enemy." In *Chicago Race Riots,* edited and compiled by Harrison George. Chicago: Great Western Publishing Co., 1919, 4–6. Marcy's contribution to a collection of articles devoted to the theme that "the cause of the race conflict in Chicago and elsewhere in the United States is rooted deep in our economic system." She argues that "When they are united the white and colored workers WIN; when the workers are divided THE BOSS WINS."

Out of the Dump." *ISR* 8 (May 1908):670–75; (June 1908):746–51; 9 (July 1908):45–50; (August 1908):106–11; (September 1908):199–204; (October 1908):266–71; (November 1908):356–61.

"The Passing of Cripple Creek." *One Big Union Monthly* 2 (April 1920);25–26. Marcy's sole contribution to the monthly published in Chicago by the executive board of the IWW from March 1919 to January 1921.

"The Passing of the Turkish Harem." *ISR* 12 (May 1912):765–67.

"The Paterson Strike." *ISR* 14 (September 1913):177–78.

"A Pickpocket." *ISR* 9 (March 1909):669–73.

"Plenty of Jobs." *ISR* 15 (April 1915):618–20.

"Power." *ISR* 16 (May 1916):691–92.

"The Power of the Railroad Boys." *ISR* 15 (May 1915):669–71.

"Progress in China." *ISR* 10 (February 1910):689–91.

"The Real Fatherland." *ISR* 15 (September 1914):177–78.

"A Revolutionary Strike Without Leaders." *ISR* 16 (August 1915):73–74.

"The Reward of Truth-Telling." *ISR* 16 (August 1915):94–96. A denunciation of economist Scott Nearing's dismissal from the University of Pennsylvania in 1915 as a consequence of his outspoken criticism of capitalism. The case was widely publicized and spurred the attempt to define the proper role and rights of the teacher.

"Run-Away Slaves." *Industrial Pioneer* 1 (July 1921):23.

"Skinny's Turkey Dinner." *ISR* 10 (November 1909):385–91.

"Socialist Unpreparedness in Germany." *ISR* 15 (October 1914):245–47.

"Song of the Swamp." In Jack Carney, *Mary Marcy.* Chicago: Charles H. Kerr & Co., 1922, 14.

"Stories of the Cave People." *ISR* 9 (April 1909):765–71; (May 1909):845–51; (June 1909):959–64; 10 (July 1909):23–31; (August 1909):144–48; (September 1909):212–19; (October 1909):327–32; 16 (March 1916):532–35; (April 1916):598–601; (May 1916):672–75; (June 1916):738–41.

"A Straw Man." *ISR* 13 (March 1913):691. A response to charges that the *ISR* encourages individual violence.

"A Strike in the 'Model Village.'" *ISR* 10 (February 1910):699–701.

"They Belong Inside!" *ISR* 17 (September 1916);146–48. Marcy is critical of the working masses' ingrained respect for the laws that capitalists use to exploit them. "Did you ever stop to consider that the present capitalist-made law . . . is no more than a Scrap of Paper *when the working class so decides?*"

"Things Doing in the Cement Industry." *ISR* 13 (July 1912):58–60.

"Through the Jungle by Rail." *ISR* 13 (November 1912):415–16.

"The Value of Immorality." *ISR* 15 (March 1915):528–29.

"Wages in Mexican Money" [A "Center Shot Leaflet"]. Chicago: Charles H. Kerr & Co., 1912. One of twenty-two booklets and leaflets issued by Kerr & Co. as its "1912 Campaign Package of Socialist Literature." The entire package, totalling four hundred pages, sold for $.25.

"We Must Fight It Out." *ISR* 15 (April 1915):627–28.

"What Will Become of Your Children?" *ISR* 12 (February 1912):473–74. An appeal for working-class mothers and fathers to think of "your children" and study Socialism and its program.

"What You Have to Sell." *ISR* 16 (September 1915):141–43.

"Where We Stand on War." *ISR* 15 (March 1915):561.

"The White Flag Agreement Brigade." *ISR* 13 (April 1913);760–62. An attack on Adolph Germer and "other pure-and-simplers" in the Socialist party for failing to support striking West Virginia coal miners. "The REVIEW and the Industrialists in the Party are with the striking miners to the bitter end of the fight. . . . We are going to help teach them the way to victory."

"Who Pays the Taxes?" *ISR* 17 (November 1916):294–96.

"Whom Do You Work For?" [A "Center Shot Leaflet"]. Chicago: Charles H. Kerr & Co., 1912. Included in Kerr & Co.'s "1912 Campaign Package of Socialist Literature."

"Whose War Is This?" *ISR* 14 (June 1914):729–31.

"Why Not Register Them All?" *ISR* 18 (August 1917):87–88.

"Why the Socialist Party Is Different." *ISR* 13 (August 1912):157.

"Why the Socialists Must 'Harp on' the Class Struggle." *Northwest Worker*, 4 November 1915.

"Why You Should Be A Socialist." *ISR* 15 (May 1915):700–702.

"William, the Faithful." *ISR* 7 (March 1907):557–58.

"Working Men and Women" [A "Center Shot Leaflet"]. Chicago: Charles H. Kerr & Co., 1912. Included in Kerr & Co.'s "1912 Campaign Package of Socialist Literature." The leaflet is an expansion of an earlier article of the same title in the *ISR* 11 (July 1910):11–12.

"The World-Wide Revolt." *ISR* 12 (November 1911):261–65.

"Your Great Adventure." *ISR* 16 (July 1915):43–46.

Index